The Official Compendium of Inner City Street Games

PAR Enterprises, Inc.

iUniverse, Inc.

New York   Bloomington

The Official Compendium of Inner City Street Games

iUniverse books may be ordered through booksellers or by contacting:

iUniverse
1663 Liberty Drive
Bloomington, IN 47403
www.iuniverse.com
1-800-Authors (1-800-288-4677)

ISBN: 978-1-4502-5411-3 (pbk)
ISBN: 978-1-4502-5412-0 (ebk)

Printed in the United States of America

iUniverse rev. date: 8/31/2010

CONTENTS

FORWARD

TESTIMONIALS

CONTENTS (CONT.)

FORWARD

Prior to the advent of video games and "virtual reality" the youth of cities such as New York, Philadelphia, Boston, Chicago, Detroit, Los Angeles, etc., relied on their creativity, "reality" and the inner city environment to produce a complement of games that were unique and specific to the inner city life. The rules and the names of these inner city street games could vary from city to city, (such as Ring-a-leevio vs. Ringolevio) but in concept they remained broadly consistent.

This compendium is dedicated to all those who, as youngsters, lived and played in city neighborhoods and the surrounding suburbs and participated in the wide array of inner city street games. Some of the games were seasonal; some were more ritual and yet others were more activities or traditional fun pastimes and were played at any time of the year. Not all were played actually in the street. "Stoops", sidewalks, curbs and sides of buildings, alley ways, school gymnasiums, vacant lots, building hallways and city parks were also required settings for some of the games. For many of the games a key requirement was the "spaldeen" (or "pinky") described in greater detail below. Additionally there were many other creative "props" and equipment, and unlike the virtual reality of today's hi-tech pastimes, the inner city street games were actual, real world and three dimensional happenings which required active participation and varied skills and agility. Volume one of this compendium describes the inner city games in terms of their setting, rules, objectives, props, and seasonality and in some instances alternative names are provided.

The **Official Compendium Of Inner City Street Games** is designed to provide a documented record and description of rules and play of the many games that were (and may continue to be) played in the streets of the inner cities of the US as experienced by the authors who were born in New York City in the 1940's and were fortunate to have played these games during their childhood and early teen years. The rules of the games would vary among cities and even among neighborhoods within a city. What is presented here is a synthesis of the more commonly recognized games and general rules that applied on a broadly consistent basis. In some cases the names of the games are spelled phonetically in the absence of an authority of consensus.

Of Importance to Schools and Youth Organizations
The Official Compendium Of Inner City Street Games is available at quantity discounts in bulk purchase for educational, promotional and fund raising purposes. For information please write to : PAR Enterprises, Inc. , 1845 Summer Street, Stamford CT 06905 or contact the company via E-mail at par@par-ent.com or toll free 1-888-333-5PAR.

SOME TESTIMONIAL PRAISE FOR

THE OFFICIAL COMPENDIUM OF INNER CITY STREET GAMES

"What a marvelous concept! As someone who spent several wonderful childhood years in the City, experiencing the extended family neighborhood, children enjoying a variety of games on streets unobstructed by parked cars or traffic, I heartily endorse this compendium of inner city games that is sure to evoke special reminiscing. Ah yes, potsy, stick ball, bouncing spaldeens, (with the accent on the latter syllable), marbles shot by champions, racing to hide in a great contest of ringalievo, running away from hard-slung stockings of flour on Thanksgiving Eve, or in some neighborhoods, on Halloween, we had it all! - as well as the neighborhood shops where penny candy, black and whites, chocolate creams, and oh, so many fountain delights were available for bottle deposits or less. ' Thanks for the memories! ' "

> *Sr. Lucille Coldrick, Principal*
> *Preston High School, Bronx,*
> *N.Y.*

"While cleaning out a closet, I came across a can full of chalk, 'scully caps', and a rumpled piece of paper depicting a game board diagram. With a reminiscent tear in my eye, I showed them to my teenage daughters and tried to explain the game of Scully to them. They looked at me with an expression that said ' why would anyone want to chase soda caps filled with melted crayons on hot pavement?' They thought I was telling a tall tale. Oddly enough, other people that I described the game to also never heard of it. Well, the soda caps were really ' crowns'. I was brought back to those hot summer days when my cousins from Jamaica, New York would visit. We would fill 'crowns' with broken crayon pieces and melt them in the sun. When our caps cooled, we would draw the playing area on the sidewalk or pavement and, with other neighborhood children, play Scully for hours. Over the years I would describe the game of Scully to people (many who grew up in the suburbs or away from the inner cities) who also never heard of this game. Today, many, many, years later, I now understand the game of Scully was an inner city game that made a visit to the 'burbs'.
The memory of this game has lasted with me all these years. What a surprise to see a variation of this game listed in this book as 'Acey Deucy' or 'killer' "

> *Letamarie Bernard*
> *Sales Executive*
> *Specialized Packaging International, Inc.*

"Thank you for taking the time to gather together the games of my youth. As I poured over the pages of your book as though flipping through an old photograph album of days gone by, visions of yesteryear flooded my mind. You brought back so many fond memories and cherished experiences.

As a boy growing up in the South Bronx, 1 took these games for granted. Now, as I read through the book I am touched and impressed by the ingenuity of these games and the imagination of their creators. We were luckier than we thought, way back then! Today, in an age of virtual reality technology and store bought games, it is hard to believe that, armed with very little, we played our hearts out and were happy. There is a lesson in there somewhere.

This wonderful book needs to be shared with the children of today. Every teacher, physical education instructor, coach, after school director and summer camp leader should have a copy of this anthology. It is filled with entertaining, imaginative and inexpensive games for children.

As an educator and former high school baseball coach in New York City, I, wholeheartedly , recommend this book to all those who work with children. Maybe the joy of being a child can be given to them through the games we once played."

Mr. Michael J. Deegan,
Principal
St. Jude School

"What a little beauty we have here in GAMES"! It was delightful just reading about what games my generation enjoyed playing on New York streets, sidewalks, and empty lots – in fact, any space where cops wouldn't chase us. It's odd to think how Mother May I reflected an era which consciously promoted respect for authority and used games to actually practice good manners. Didn't Ringo Livio spawn heroes and heroines who would sacrifice themselves for the freedom of others! Remember?

After having worked 39 years in New York City public schools and day camps, I can frankly state that the proper and timely introduction of some of these games during the regular and summer school seasons would provide delightfully creative, wholesome and enjoyable ways of assisting schools to fulfill the fundamental aims and objectives of education: i.e.,

- *CHARACTER. Children experience increased self-reliance and self-direction when playing such games as Dodgeball or Running Bases? In an argument, we all learned to accept the fact that there were many differences of opinion. But, we learned to admire the good sportsmanship shown when an adverse judgment against the opposing team was called by the "ump" and accepted, and vice versa. Don't we promote fair play when we follow the rules of the game instead of bullying others into submission? But when we were unfairly bullied, didn't we learn early on that there were degrees of goodness and badness in others?*
- *OUR AMERICAN HERITAGE. The games we played promoted respect for the dignity and worth of individuals regardless of race, religion or anything else when we let "them" play with us and learned how terrific some of those kids really were. And didn't some of us form fast friendships that have survived the test of time?*
- *HEALTH. Games like Basketball One-on-One, help develop a sound body and wholesome attitudes and habits for enjoyment in both present and future leisure times? Who doesn't chuckle observing the commercials highlighting Michael Jordan with that other man who always misses the basket or the commercial featuring the father whose wife suggests he take supplementary nutrition to keep up with his son in a series of one-on-one basketball games? What activity could surpass the required concentration, perseverance and coordination necessary to participate in such activities as Jump Rope, Double Dutch, Handball or Boxball Baseball? Whose heart is not moved by the obvious sense of personal worth evident on the face of the little child in the wheelchair who became the Noc Hockey champion at camp or summer school?*
- *KNOWLEDGE AND SKILLS. Didn't we learn and profit by listening to the teacher or coach, our big brother or sister or the kid who was a great player?*
- *THINKING. Children developed good judgment in selecting group leaders and captains who in turn had to pick others. As GAMES states, "Many choices and careful decisions had to be made at the beginning of most games." . It wasn't uncommon for team games to be won or lost in the choosing process. GAMES shows that one must succeed in thinking fast on one's feet to win.*

- *APPRECIATION AND EXPRESSION. In "Spaldeen" Ball Bounce girls learned to sing rote songs and respond to fundamental rhythms and rhymes synchronized to the bouncing ball. Children show impressive originality and inventiveness resulting in the creation of many variations in GAMES.*
- *SOCIAL RELATIONSHIPS. We know today that desirable social attitudes and relationships were formed—some of them for life. Didn't the street games and pastimes mentioned in GAMES give us our earliest lessons in following simple, understandable and fair rules.*
- *ECONOMIC RELATIONSHIPS. We kids developed an awareness and appreciation of economic realities and the significance of money when we learned that we could play with the big boys **only** if we brought that expensive, prized sports equipment we owned which they so desired!*

This is a book of games and pastimes many of which originated on the street and the one thing you could always count on in the street was having fun. The best of us weren't always "goody-goodies". There were Carpet Guns and Peashooters which we called "puddy-blowers". Money was scarce during the Great Depression. Since Mom and Dad were never keen on these little weapons, they couldn't spend good money on dried peas to be blown away on kid's games! Nature came to the rescue by providing – free of charge – small round green wild cherries which, when in season, determined the opening of our "hunting season". But all this wasn't that bad considering the fact that many of us grew up in an era when cops were universally considered "good guys" and guns were used by millions of Americans to rid the world of Nazi tyranny.

Out of school, this anthology of games and pastimes provides a chance for fathers, mothers, big brothers and sisters to explore the contents of this published jewel, to teach rules and regulations, and perhaps, to share even now, a few of the games that provided some of the most thrilling and memorable moments of our youth.

James W. Salta, Assistant Principal (Retired)
Charles R. Drew Intermediate School #148
The Bronx, New York

<u>About the Authors</u>

Dr. Paul A. Rivera and Letty, his wife, were born around the end of World War II in New York City. They attended Sts. Peter & Paul grammar school, Paul attended Cardinal Hayes High School and Manhattan College where he received a degree in electrical engineering. He subsequently completed his MBA and doctoral degree in Finance from Pace University. He married his childhood sweetheart, Letty, who also enjoyed the inner city street games and attended Sts Peter & Paul, Cathedral High and the College of Mt. St. Vincent. Dr. Rivera manages a consulting practice and is a professor at local universities.. He was formerly Director of Benefits for American Brands, Inc. and for the prior 25 years worked with the Xerox Corporation and GTE International, Inc. . He has authored other business publications but in this book Paul & Letty describe with fondness the simple and creative rules of play that they enjoyed as a youngsters. Paul recalls his earlier years living in the Bronx as being encompassed by three major endeavors, i.e. 1) school 2) working in his father's grocery store on weekends (where many of the "props" for the games were bought by the neighborhood kids) and 3) playing the wonderful games described herein.

SPALDEEN BALL BOUNCE

TYPE/CATEGORY: BALL BOUNCE - TYPICALLY BY GIRLS

SETTING: SIDEWALK OR PARK GROUNDS

REQUIREMENTS: CONCRETE OR ASPHALT HARD PAVED FLOOR, A SPALDEEN BALL, ONE OR MORE PLAYERS

OBJECTIVE: TO BOUNCE A BALL TO A SONG, IN CADENCE, TO A RHYME, WITHOUT MISSING

DESCRIPTION: The idea of this ball bouncing game was to stand erect and bounce a ball vertical between the ground and hand. The ball was typically a spaldeen which was a hollow rubber ball, pink in color and about the same size and weight of a tennis ball but without the fuzzy texture. The surface was smooth. The game could be played by one or more kids. The idea was to see how many times the ball could be bounced without missing. A way of measuring this was to sing a song or call out a rhyme or cadence song the lyrics of which coincided with each bounce. The rhyme would progress alphabetically to indicate how far the player was able to bounce the ball without missing. The player would lose their turn when missing a bounce and would need to start over from the beginning of the rhyme at the next turn. The first player to complete the alphabet would win the first round and then progress to a second round of the alphabet but with added challenge. Added challenge included such things as crossing one's leg over the ball or clapping once or twice as the ball bounced back up from the floor.

One popular rhyme went as follows: "   ...'A' ..my name is Alice and my husband's name is Albert and we come from Alabama and we make apples,...'B' ..my name is Betty and my husband's name is Bob and we come from Brooklyn and we make bubbles...."....and so on, in this example the ball was bounced on almost each word, excepting the articles and prepositions. The bouncing was kept at a steady pace while performing the required action and the ball would need to hit the ground in rhythm with the first letter of the key word.

SPALDEEN BOUNCE

One popular rhyme went as follows: "   ...'A' ..my name is Alice and my husband's name is Albert and we come from Alabama and we make apples,...'B' ..my name is Betty and my husband's name is Bob and we come from Brooklyn and we make bubbles...."....and so on

ACE BOX BALL ("SLUG")

TYPE/CATEGORY: FORM OF SHORT RANGE OPEN-HAND, HANDBALL

SETTING: SIDEWALK AGAINST A BUILDING WALL

REQUIREMENTS: CEMENT SIDEWALK ADJACENT TO THE SMOOTH VERTICAL WALL OF A BUILDING, TWO OR MORE PLAYERS.

OBJECTIVE: TO ELIMINATE PLAYERS BY HITTING A SPALDEEN BALL TO OTHER PLAYERS OFF THE WALL, BUT CLOSE TO THE GROUND AND WITH ONE BOUNCE BETWEEN THE PLAYER AND WALL

DESCRIPTION: Essential props to this game were the engraved lines on cement sidewalks that marked off the cement surface into squares of about 4 foot sides. Sidewalk surface cracks were a problem obstacle. Up to about 5 or more players would stand side by side and facing the building wall at a distance of about 2 to 4 "sidewalk squares" from the wall. For most sidewalks, this would place the players close to the curb. The 2 to 4 squares in line and in front of the player, between the player and the wall, represented the player's "playing field" or area. Any ball hit into the player's area had to be returned within one bounce to another player's area. The first player to the left (the "Ace") would serve hitting the ball with an open underhand serve with one bounce up against the wall and into another player's play area. To the right of the Ace stood the King, then the Queen, then the Jack (as in picture cards). The serve had to bounce once before hitting the wall. The bounce could be into any other player's area. The player of the area into which the ball bounced on the rebound had to hit the ball back against the wall also within one bounce. The ball could be hit into any player's row. The players continued hitting until a player missed. The ball was kept at less than two feet from the ground during play. Playing the ball low, hard and fast and with spin was a way of causing other players to miss. Once a player missed such player would move to the end of the row of players at the right and lose a point. Players would determine how many points (typically 10) would eliminate the player from the game and therefore leaving one less player in the row. Alternatively, the last player in the row to the right would be automatically eliminated on his/her first missed point (choosing was a critical aspect with this rule). If the ball rebounded bouncing diagonally out of a player's area and not within the player's reach, it could be "saved" by the adjacent player if hit back to the wall within one bounce. The "saved" player would retain their position in the row and not lose the point. If the "Ace" (server) missed a ball hit into the server's area, he or she would drop to the end of the row but not lose a point. So another objective was to "dethrone" the "Ace" server and obtain and hold the serving position as long as possible. The ball would be served again by the "Ace" server every time other players would miss. Players moving to the end of the row would cause each of the other players to shift one playing area to the left. As players were eliminated, the number of remaining players would drop. A great spectator sport when the game was down to 2 players trying to eliminate each other. Having a low, fast and hard "killer" serve was a thrilling advantage.

ACE BOX BALL – "SLUG"

Having a low, fast and hard "killer" serve was a thrilling advantage.

RUNNING BASES

TYPE/CATEGORY: RUNNING AND BALL TOSS

SETTING: CITY STREET BETWEEN TWO MANHOLE COVERS

REQUIREMENTS: SPALDEEN BALL, BASEBALL GLOVES (OPTIONAL), AT LEAST THREE PLAYERS

OBJECTIVE: TO RUN BETWEEN TWO MANHOLE COVERS (BASES) WITHOUT BEING TAGGED BY THE BALL THROWER OR BALL CATCHER STANDING AT EACH BASE.

DESCRIPTION: The game required at least three players. Two of the players each would "cover" a base, or stand at or near one of the manhole covers which were typically about 100 feet apart in the middle of the street. This was more of a challenge between the runners and the ball throwers. The play was similar to the situation in regular baseball, when a runner gets caught between bases and can be chased or tagged with the ball by defensive players at either base.

The object of the game was to see how many times the runner (s) could make it between bases without getting caught or tagged by one of the two defensive players at either base. An alternative way of scoring was to count each successful run to the other base as a baseball "run".

The offensive player(s) would stand on the base (or either base in the event of more than one runner). The defensive players would throw the ball back and forth between each other, encouraging the runners to make a break for the opposite base. Once a runner moved out into the open, the defensive players would attempt to put a "squeeze" on the runner. They could close in on the runner in an attempt to tag the runner. The runner could dodge the ball thrower if a tag was attempted, but only within certain boundaries (i.e. running up on the sidewalk and behind the cars to get to other base was not in the rules). If a player was tagged that player would then switch places with the tagging player and the tagging player would become a new runner.

Rules varied, for example with 4 or more players, two teams could be set up as runners were tagged they would sit out the round until the remaining team members were tagged. Once all the players of a team were tagged out, the teams would switch roles and the ball throwers would cover the bases for the defensive team. Defensive/running positions were determined by the "choosing" ritual described elsewhere.

Fast feet, sharp/fast body moves, a good eye, a fast ball and effective faking of the throw were all essential ploys of the game.

BASES

Fast feet, sharp/fast body moves, a good eye, a fast ball and effective faking of the throw were all essential ploys of the game

BASEBALL CARDS (TRADING)

TYPE/CATEGORY: ENTERPRISE

SETTING: ON STOOPS, IN HALLWAYS, AT HOME, IN THE PARK, VIRTUALLY ANYWHERE

REQUIREMENTS: AT LEAST TWO PLAYERS, EACH WITH A CORRESPONDING SET OF BASEBALL PICTURE CARDS

OBJECTIVE: TO TRADE BASEBALL PICTURE CARDS

DESCRIPTION: This was more a ritual rather than a game. In those days baseball cards were mostly acquired through trading in the "secondary" market,..i.e...the primary market was the candy store, where the cards were initially acquired in a pack with a stick or piece of chewing gum for a nickel. Baseball cards at that time,...i.e. prior to the 1970's were not popular in pre-packaged collectors sets. They were a commodity of fun and amusement rather than of value as they became in the 1980's. The trading was typically among the young males. The traders would meet either in a hallway of a building or on the stoop and deliberate at length as to the worth of the cards. The idea was to get a favorite or desired card, match or complete a team, collect a full roster of a team or a league for a particular position, i.e. the full pitching line up for the Yanks or all the first basemen for the American league,...etc..of course owning the card of a popular player or record holder was of value. Statistics were important. Cards were traded for many of the above reasons. The value of the card was recognized by the number of cards it would bring in return. A "300" batter obviously would require easily two or three "250' batters and so on. The criteria varied and so did the motivation. At times to complete a line up (like all the pitchers of a team) a trader would be willing to let go of an otherwise more valuable card in a one for one deal. Other "sweeteners" at times could be included, such as some change, gum, etc. Many times extensive negotiations included comic books and other commodities.

BASEBALL CARDS (TRADING)

In those days baseball cards were mostly acquired through trading in the "secondary" market,..i.e...the primary market was the candy store, where the cards were initially acquired in a pack with a stick or piece of chewing gum for a nickel.

BASEBALL CARDS -FLIPPING

TYPE/CATEGORY: CARD GAME

SETTING: IN THE HALLWAYS, STOOPS OR NEAR A WALL

REQUIREMENTS: AT LEAST TWO PLAYERS, EACH WITH A CORRESPONDING SET OF BASEBALL PICTURE CARDS

OBJECTIVE: TO ACCUMULATE AS MANY OF THE OTHER PLAYER'S BASEBALL PICTURE CARDS AS POSSIBLE

DESCRIPTION: The players would stand next to a wall and hold a card with either the face or back parallel to the ground about three to four feet from the floor. The card would be held perpendicular to and up against the wall. In alternating turns the players would let a baseball card drop. On the way to the floor, the cards would flip in the air turning a number of times before hitting the ground. Depending on whether the card landed face up or down, it either remained in play or it won the round for its player. A common version went as follows: the starting player would flip the first card. If the card landed face up (or down), then the player of the next card landing face up(or down) would collect all of the cards on the ground. For example, assume that the first card flipped had landed face up and that the next four flipped cards all had landed face down. The sixth card landing face up would win all six cards for the corresponding player. The rewards matched the risks. As could be appreciated, players would reserve their less valuable "trades" for card flipping. An alternative way of flipping was simply to flip the cards on to the ground from about waist high by hand.

In another version of the game the cards were flipped towards the base of a wall about four feet away. The player whose card landed closest to the wall without actually touching the wall would win the cards that were tossed by the other players in that round. This version was similar to the game of "pitching pennies" or coins as described later. And as expected only the run down or crummy cards were risked in this game. The flipping of the cards required some wrist action and technique. The best way to get distance on the card and avoid drag was to hold the card between index finger and thumb at one of its corners. The card would be held either face down or face up and parallel to the ground then flipped like a "frisbee" towards the base of the wall.

BASEBALL CARDS -FLIPPING

As could be appreciated, players would reserve their less valuable "trades" for card flipping.

BASKETBALL - 1 ON 1

TYPE/CATEGORY: BASKETBALL

SETTING: CITY PARK OR SCHOOL YARD PLAYGROUND

REQUIREMENTS: TWO PLAYERS , A BASKETBALL, AND "SNEAKERS" ($5/pair)

OBJECTIVE: TO SCORE THE MOST BASKETBALL GOALS

DESCRIPTION: The game was played by two players either at a "school yard" or a city park/playground basketball court. The playgrounds or school yards many times had only one basketball hoop. Basketball rules were applied in broadly consistent fashion. When the game was played by only two players or "one on one", the game was a fast paced one. Points were either scored in the conventional manner (2 points to a goal) or single points to a goal. The simple version of "one on one" was merely that of being able to rebound and take as many shots as possible. Some specific rules were applied because of the various aspects of the game. For example, to maintain the pace of the game at a reasonable level upon rebounding the other player's missed shot, the player in possession would need to dribble the ball back out past the foul line before attempting to shoot. This was not required when a player rebounded his own shot. In many cases the court was not complete or to regulation. Boundaries were established as needed. Upon scoring a goal, the scoring player would resume play from the boundary line somewhere behind the foul line (typically a half court line). The most popular shots were the jump shot, hook shot, the lay up and the "set up' shot. The "set up" shot was a mutually accepted free shot from some distance. If the ball handler was being effectively covered/guarded by the defensive player and was not able to continue dribbling (to avoid a "double dribble") the offensive player would request a "set" shot. If the offensive player agreed, then he could position himself back under the basket for the rebound and the shooting player would have to shoot from his outer position. The offensive player would be willing to give up the free rebound in the event of a missed shot, for a "free" unguarded shot. The defensive player's stake was a free shot for the opponent player in exchange for an easy rebound should the shooter miss the point. The goal hoops rarely "sported" a net. Good faking, rebounding, consistency from under the net were key to the game.

BASKETBALL - 1 ON 1

Good faking, rebounding, consistency from under the net were key to the game.

BASKETBALL (FIVE-TWO)

TYPE/CATEGORY: BASKETBALL

SETTING: CITY PARK OR SCHOOL YARD PLAYGROUND

REQUIREMENTS: TWO OR MORE PLAYERS

OBJECTIVE: TO SCORE THE MOST BASKETBALL GOALS

DESCRIPTION: This version of basketball was played by two or more individual players as opposed to two teams. As in "one on one" the game was played at half court or with only one goal. The players took turns at scoring baskets. The object of the game was to be the highest scoring individual player. Points were scored either from the foul line or from the rebound position as follows. Players would choose their starting order. In turn each player would be permitted up to two shots. The first shot would be from the foul line. If the foul line shot was good, five points were scored. After shooting from the foul line the player would rebound the ball and would take a second shot from the rebound position. Shots from the rebound position scored two points. The second shot had to be made from wherever the player caught the ball on the rebound and no further steps or dribbling towards the basket from that rebound position was permitted. Missing the foul line shot and hitting the rim of the hoop could cause the ball to bounce high and far from the hoop making the second shot more difficult. If both the foul line shot and the rebound shot were scored (for 7 points) the player would take another turn for two more shots and continue until he missed either the foul line or rebound shot of a turn. If a player's foul line shot missed or did not hit the hoop/rim or backboard, the rebound shot was forfeited ending his turn. The winning score was set at the beginning, typically the first player to score 36 points was declared the winner. The remaining players could continue to compete for second , third place etc. Having a consistent and accurate foul line shot was key in addition to moving fast on the rebound (to keep the second shot as close to the hoop as possible).

BASKETBALL (FIVE-TWO)

Having a consistent and accurate foul line shot was key in addition to moving fast on the rebound (to keep the second shot as close to the hoop as possible).

BASKETBALL - DONKEY

TYPE/CATEGORY: BASKETBALL

SETTING: CITY PARK OR SCHOOL YARD PLAYGROUND

REQUIREMENTS: TWO OR MORE PLAYERS

OBJECTIVE: TO ELIMINATE THE REMAINING PLAYERS BY CONSISTENTLY SCORING BASKETS AS DESCRIBED

DESCRIPTION: This version of basketball was also played by two or more individual players as opposed to two teams. Only one goal or half court was required. The players would choose their starting positions and would play in turn as follows. The first player would attempt to score a basket from any position on the court and using any type of shot the player chose (i.e. jump shot, hook shot, lay up, set shot, etc.). If the player scored a basket, then the following player would be required to attempt the same shot from the same location. If the second player scored the basket then the next player would be required to attempt the same shot and conditions and so on until a player in sequence missed the shot. However, if the first player did not score his basket it was up to the next player to establish the shot to be duplicated by the rest until someone in turn missed the duplicated shot. During the round, each successive player would have to attempt the same shot and conditions as long as the preceding player had duplicated and scored the shot. Failing to score a basket that had been scored by all the preceding players resulted in a lost point i.e. the player would be penalized with a letter from the word "donkey". The first time a player missed a required shot he received the letter "d", the second loss corresponded to the letter "o" and so on until the player had accumulated all the letters of the word "donkey". Accumulating all the letters of the word "donkey" eliminated the player from the game. If all the players in a round scored or successfully duplicated the required shot, then upon his next turn, the player that had established the required shot for duplication, could attempt a different type of shot and from anywhere on the court. However, if during the round a player missed the shot (and was penalized with a letter) the player following the penalized player would not have to duplicate the shot and could establish a new shot of his own choosing. If this player was successful in scoring a basket then the scored shot would have to be duplicated by succeeding players until someone missed. If the remaining players all scored the duplicated shot, then upon his next turn, the player originating the scored basket could then take any other type of shot (or the same one if he so chose). Players would lose points and accumulate letters only when missing or failing to duplicate a shot that had been scored by preceding players as long as he had not been the originator of the shot to be duplicated. If the preceding player missed a shot that had previously been in duplication mode, then the next player could establish the new shot to be duplicated. In attempting to establish a new shot, if the player missed, this would not count as a loss. The opportunity to establish the required shot was only passed to the next player. Only missing a shot that was in duplication mode was a loss. Missing the basket when trying to set up a new shot for others to duplicate (because the prior player had missed a required shot) did not correspond to a lost point. Scoring trick shots and fancy maneuvers at times made the game interesting because such would have to be duplicated by the succeeding players when a basket was scored. Typically the two best players would end up as finalists. It was interesting to see the two remaining players battle to eliminate each other with creative moves and shots.

BASKETBALL - DONKEY
Scoring trick shots and fancy maneuvers at times made the game interesting because such would have to be duplicated by the succeeding players when a basket was scored.............. It was interesting to see the two remaining players battle to eliminate each other with creative moves and shots.

BOX BALL BASEBALL

TYPE/CATEGORY: SIDEWALK BALL GAME

SETTING: CITY SIDEWALK

REQUIREMENTS: TWO PLAYERS

OBJECTIVE: TO SCORE THE MOST "RUNS" IN NINE INNINGS BY "PITCHING" A SPALDEEN AS DESCRIBED.

DESCRIPTION: Two players would stand facing each other about four or five sidewalk cement squares apart. These were the squares engraved on the concrete surface of sidewalks with 3 to 4 foot sides. The game emulated the game of baseball to the extent that nine innings were played with six outs to an inning (3 for each player). However the way that the runs, hits, strikes and outs were scored was quite different. Players would choose the beginning offensive or defensive positions. The defensive player (the pitcher) would stand directly facing the four or five in line sidewalk squares in front of him slightly leaning forward, but could not step into the box immediately in front of him. Alternatively, the player could sort of straddle either corner of the box nearest him. The idea was to lean into the box immediately in front of him without stepping into or falling into the box. This box would become the "infield" box in that the batter would need to hit into this box at least on a first bounce to score a hit. As described below the offensive player or batter would stand facing the pitcher at the other end of the row of four or five boxes away. The batter also could not step into the box immediately in front of him. The box in front of the batter was the pitch box, and the pitcher would have to pitch the spaldeen into this box on one bounce. The pitcher would pitch the spaldeen, underhand, into the pitch box on one bounce, i.e. the pitched ball would need to first bounce in the box immediately in front of the batter. The batter would need to hit the ball after the one bounce, with an open hand, back into the infield box in front of the pitcher. To score as a hit, the ball would have to bounce first into the infield box. If the pitcher was able to lean far enough into the infield box and catch the hit ball on the fly before it bounced in the infield box, the caught fly ball would count as an out. If the hit ball bounced once in the infield box before it was caught on the rebound, the bounce scored as a single. If the ball bounced two or three or four times before it was caught, the subsequent bounces would score as a double, triple, or home run respectively. Bounces subsequent to the first bounce did not have to be in the infield box. These subsequent bounces could be any where outside of the playing boxes. The bounces ("hits") from subsequent pitches would advance the prior men on bases. For example two single bounces in sequence would result with a man on first and a man on second. If the batter missed the pitch or if the hit ball did not bounce first in the infield box a strike was counted. The players would keep their corresponding positions when a side was retired with three outs. The boxes immediately in front of each player reversed, i.e. the pitch box then became the infield box for the other player and the infield box became the pitch box for the opposing pitcher. Effective defensive ploys included fast under hand pitching with spin on the ball. The spaldeen was compliant and with appropriate "English" upon release the pitched ball could be bounced with back, forward or side spin. Back spin would result in a thwarted/short bounce. Forward or top spin would cause the ball to take off after the bounce. Side spin would cause the ball to bounce off to the side. A skillful pitcher could combine more than one of these pitches to throw off and strike out the batter. The offensive ploy, on the other hand, was to have a keen eye and a fast open hand slap on the ball. A ball hit low and fast into the infield box was not easy to catch. This would minimize balls caught on the fly before bouncing and at times could cause the pitcher to miss or fumble the ball after the first bounce, increasing the chance of multiple bounces for a home run.

 Another version of box ball had as an objective keeping the ball in play within a two square box area which contained four boxes. At each of the four corners a player would stand. The ball was played between the boxes with one bounce per box. The players would return a ball from their corresponding box into another player's box. Only one bounce was permitted within the player's box. If the ball was bounced into a player's box he or she would have to hit the ball on one bounce and return the ball into another player's box hitting the ball with an open hand. Missing the ball or allowing it to bounce more than once in your box resulted in a point loss.

BOX BALL BASEBALL

Effective defensive ploys included fast under hand pitching with spin on the ball. The spaldeen was compliant and with appropriate "English" upon release the pitched ball could be bounced with back, forward or side spin. Back spin would result in a thwarted/short bounce. Forward or top spin would cause the ball to take off after the bounce. Side spin would cause the ball to bounce off to the side.

CARPET GUNS

TYPE/CATEGORY: GADGETRY

SETTING: CITY STREETS

REQUIREMENTS: CLOTHES PIN, WOOD PIECES, RUBBER BAND, TAPE , TACKS, PIECES OF LINOLEUM FLOOR COVERING

OBJECTIVE: TO CONSTRUCT THE FARTHEST SHOOTING CARPET GUN

DESCRIPTION: Some neighborhood activities required some construction and engineering know how. The carpet gun was a device that was individually built by the owner to his own specifications. The device would shoot pieces of linoleum carpet floor covering at great distances. The pieces were cut to about one inch squares. They were propelled by the release of a stretched rubber band which was mounted and loaded on the device as described below. First, the stock of the gun was constructed by nailing or taping two pieces of wood in an "L" shape to resemble a pistol. At the front end of the gun the end of a heavy rubber band was tacked. At the other end of the gun near the rear and on top (about where the hammer of a pistol would normally be located) a clothes pin was tacked or taped. Clothes pins were used to hang laundry for drying on a clothes line. Of the two common types in use at that time one had a fixed opening and it would be forced on the clothesline to hold the clothing. The other was a spring loaded pin. It was a normally closed pin kept shut under the pressure of a spring that joined two pieces of wood as a clamp. The clothes pin had to be opened by squeezing the ends together. The spring loaded type was used in the carpet gun. It was mounted on the top of the gun near the "hammer" end with the clamp end facing forward. Of the two sections of the pin clamp, only the lower section, which touched the gun, was taped or tacked to the gun. This would leave the top section free to open and close like a clamp. The gun was loaded by placing a piece of linoleum inside the free end of the rubber band and then stretching the end with the carpet piece back over the top of the gun and into the clamp of the clothes pin. Care had to be taken to avoid an accidental "discharge' while loading. Once loaded, the gun could be aimed and fired by pressing down on the clothespin with the thumb. This would release the stretched rubber band and propel the flat piece of carpet through the air. The carpet pieces were loaded with the flat sides parallel to the horizon. When fired they would be projected through the air with a spinning/rotating motion similar to that of a Frisbee or discus in flight. When properly loaded into a well made carpet gun, a one inch square piece of linoleum carpet could easily be shot 100 to 200 feet. Caution was required to guard against misuse or injury. The idea was to see who could shoot the farthest.

<u>CHALKED SOCKS (Halloween)</u>

TYPE/CATEGORY: SEASONAL,

TRADITIONAL PRACTICE

SETTING: INNER CITY

REQUIREMENTS: OLD SOCK, DIFFERENT COLORED CHALK

OBJECTIVE: KIDS WOULD SMACK EACH OTHER WITH THE SOCKS TO CHALK UP THEIR CLOTHING.

DESCRIPTION: This was more of a seasonal activity of individual mischief on Halloween. The kids would chase each other through the streets in a game of "tag" swinging their socks like a medieval mace and pelting each other. The idea was to leave as much powdered chalk or flour on the other kid's clothing. You wore your worst clothing on that day. The best sock would be a man's knee high dress sock. Some used a woman's nylon stocking. The socks were filled with either crushed chalk of any color or baking flour. Alternatively a mixture of both could be used. The chalk was prepared by filling the toe of the sock with a handful sticks of chalk. The chalk inside the sock was then crushed into a powder by either hitting the filled toe of the sock with a blunt object or by smacking the sock up against the side of a building or any hard surface. Sometimes a compound mixture of chalk and flour could be used. The resulting chalk/flour powder would be released through the sock fabric upon impact leaving powder stains on clothing or any other target. Flour was already a much finer powdery compound which would leave more of a mark upon impact. Colored chalk in addition to the standard white was also popular, particularly if one was fortunate to have located a few big thick sticks, about five times the diameter of standard classroom chalk. The unsuspecting kid returning home from school in the afternoon in their school attire was a "dead duck" and easily the victim of other kids who had made it home quicker in time to change and load up their Halloween socks. The following day was an economic boom for laundries, dry cleaning stores, and probably the highest single day consumption of "FAB" and "NEW BLUE CHEER".

CHALKED SOCKS

The unsuspecting kid returning home from school in the afternoon in their school attire was a "dead duck" and easily the victim of other kids who had made it home quicker in time to change and load up their Halloween socks.

<u>CHOOSING</u>

TYPE/CATEGORY: REQUIRED SPORTS RITUAL

SETTING: THE CORRESPONDING GAME SETTING

REQUIREMENTS: TWO TEAM REPRESENTATIVES

OBJECTIVE: IT WAS A PROCESS FOR DETERMINING THE ORDER OR TURN AT PLAY, POSITION, TEAM MEMBERS AND OTHER GAME CHOICES

DESCRIPTION: Choosing was probably the single most essential aspect at the beginning of many games. Many choices and careful decisions had to be made at the beginning of most games. In team sports, the two team captains were self appointed with group consensus and typically one was the owner of the ball or other required equipment. For team games the two captains would first choose for first pick of team members, i.e. the captain winning the "choosing" process got first pick and then alternate picks with the other captain. Being one of the last to be chosen could be an ego-deflating embarrassment. The team captains would then choose again for the choice of either defensive or offensive field positions. Choosing was required in other games. Such as in Ace or Slug, where the choosing process determined the Ace, King, Queen, etc. positions as described previously. Choosing was needed also to determine the beginning anchor player in other games where one individual coordinated the game for all other players as in "red light green light" described later. The choosing process was very ritualized and took various forms. One form was the "odd man out" approach. This was a choosing by elimination. For example, five players would stand facing each other in a circle with their hands behind their backs.. One of the players would cue the players with a call out such as "one strikes three shoot". On cue the players would thrust their right hand into the circle displaying either one or two open fingers. A player was eliminated from the choosing process if his one or two fingers was at odds with the other players, i.e. if one player held two fingers open while all the others held one, that player was eliminated. Depending on the game being played, the order or turn of play would correspond to their order of elimination. For example, the first to be eliminated would be the fifth player, the second player eliminated would be the fourth turn player and so on. When the choosing was down to two players the following process was used. The players would each select either "odds" or "evens" , i.e. one player would select "odds" and the other "evens". Then on cue, they would thrust out either one open or two open fingers. The sum of their fingers would be either even (a two or a four) or odd (a three). Some choosers permitted a closed fist as a zero which probably increased the statistical equity of the process. The players would continue the hand thrusts until the first of three odd sums or three even sums was counted. If three odd sums resulted before three even sums then the "odds" player won the choosing, and was the first turn player, or had first pick of players, etc. Alternative choosing methods included coin tossing ("heads or tails"). Another unique choosing ritual when a baseball or stick ball bat was handy went as follows. One player would hold the bat vertically and release it up in the air just above shoulder level. The second player would catch the bat with one hand before it hit the ground. The idea was to catch the bat at about its mid section. With the player that caught the bat still holding the bat vertically the first player would grasp the bat with one directly above the hand of the other. Then hand over hand the players would alternately grasp the bat up to the top. The player to get the last grasp would win the choosing. In some situations there would remain an exposed section of the top of the bat, too small for a full hand grasp but enough for a player to "palm" the top of the bat with a closed hand. In this situation, the player clutching the top of the bat would hold it at that point vertically and away from his body with his arm out-stretched at about shoulder height. The other player would release his grasp and attempt to win the choosing by knocking the bat from the player's clutch with three kicks to the bat. The player in possession of the bat would win the choose if he was able to hold on to the bat during the three kicks. Another version required the holder of the bat to twirl the bat in a circular motion three times around his body before the opposing team captain attempted to kick the bat out of his hand. As an alternative, and when less than a full hand grip was left near the top of the bat, the players would reach the top by grasping with "scissor fingers" .

CHOOSING

Choosing was probably the single most essential aspect at the beginning of many games. Many choices and careful decisions had to be made at the beginning of most games. In team sports, the two team captains were self appointed with group consensus and typically one was the owner of the ball or other required equipment.

DODGE BALL

TYPE/CATEGORY: BALL TOSSING

SETTING: SCHOOL YARD OR OPEN AREA BETWEEN FACING WALLS ABOUT 100 FEET APART

REQUIREMENTS: TWO TEAMS AND A BASKETBALL OR SIMILAR SIZE LIGHTER BALL

OBJECTIVE: TO ELIMINATE THE OPPOSING TEAM BY TOSSING AND HITTING THEM WITH A BALL.

DESCRIPTION: Two teams would be set up from about fifty to one hundred feet apart, facing each other parallel to each other and to the walls behind them. The walls were not always necessary but if available they would act as a stop or back up for the ball and minimized ball chasing. At times only one wall was available and the opposing team would play in the open. The idea of the game was to throw the ball at the facing team members and tag any part of a team member with the ball. If a player was tagged or hit by an incoming ball, such player would fall out of the team's line up and was eliminated from further play. The ball could be thrown on a fly or on the ground. Throwing on a fly had both advantages and disadvantages. Under some rules, if a fly ball was caught by an opposing team member the throwing player would be eliminated. However the fly throw was faster and at times was the most effective way of hitting the target. Fly balls were not thrown high and with an arc but were thrown just above body height and with the pull of gravity, a good throw would hit the opposing players somewhere below waist or knee level. The ground ball throw was not as fast but at times, if thrown fast could take a couple of bounces and catch a player's feet or legs. The most effective throw was a fast throw that would bounce just in front of the target player hitting the legs or feet. (thus avoiding a catch but having the speed of a fly ball). The teams would alternate throwing the ball. The receiving team would have to either dodge the ball to prevent a hit or attempt to catch a fly ball. Slower players were eliminated earlier in the game and those with quick feet and good reflexes would last longer. At the start of the game it was easier to eliminate players because of the greater number of target players, even a misdirected throw could tag an unintended target player. One strategy would be to not look at the target player and fake the throw to another target player or to throw the ball diagonally or in a direction other than directly in front. The game got more difficult as players were eliminated. When it was down to two players, and typically the best and hardest throwers, the idea was to aim directly for the players legs or feet with a fast low fly or with a short bounce just in front of the player before hitting. If the player's were good they could risk a fast fly directly to the other player on the hope that the player would attempt to catch the ball and fail. Dropping an attempted catch would be scored as a hit and eliminate that player.

DODGE BALL

The most effective throw was a fast throw that would bounce just in front of the target player hitting the legs or feet. (thus avoiding a catch but having the speed of a fly ball).

FIRE SWITCH

TYPE/CATEGORY: PASTIME

SETTING: ON SIDEWALK

REQUIREMENTS: 5 PLAYERS

OBJECTIVE: TO OCCUPY AND KEEP A CORNER POSITION

DESCRIPTION: The game was similar to musical chairs in that there was one more player than the number of positions to be occupied. By losing in the choosing, a fifth player would stand in the middle of the play area which consisted of a square comprised of two sidewalk squares on each side. The other four players would each occupy one of the outer corners of the larger square. The outer corners were about two arms lengths away and so the corner players could reach the arm of another corner player. The middle player would call out the word "fire". On this cue the corner players would switch their corners. This was done with a diagonal or cross corner. The corner players would stealthily signal each other with winks or otherwise prior to switching corners. If in the process the middle player was able to capture a corner being switched by stepping on such before any other player, then the odd out player would assume the center position and the game would continue. Players would bluff or fake a switch to throw off the middle player, while the real switch took place at another end of the square. Strong arms, a long stride, a bluffing a switch were key to the game.

FIRE SWITCH

The middle player would call out the word "fire". On this cue the corner players would switch their corners.

FLIES ARE UP

TYPE/CATEGORY: BALL BATTING

SETTING: SCHOOL YARD, PARK, FIELD/LOT, OR STREET

REQUIREMENTS: AT LEAST THREE PLAYERS, A STICK BALL BAT, SPALDEEN, BASEBALL GLOVES

OBJECTIVE: TO REMAIN AT BAT OR HAVE MANY AT BATS BY CATCHING FLY BALLS

DESCRIPTION: The game was an individual rather than team play but was best with at least three players. It was mostly played in an open field, lot , city playground or on the streets. Most of the street games played literally on the streets were structured and designed to conform to the layout of the street. Side streets, having minimal car traffic were best. Rarely were the actual street games played on the main, larger and busy streets. The side streets were at times relatively narrow as compared to a ball field. A typical side street was the width of one car lane plus two parking lanes on either side. The three lane width was then flanked by sidewalks on both sides of the street, and the rules, depending on the game, varied. "Flies are up" was best played in an open lot or ball field. If played in a narrower side street fly balls caught after bouncing off of a car or a fire escape, or a building wall were valid catches. The idea of the game was for the batter to hit balls out to the field. The field players would attempt to catch all the balls. When a fly ball was caught the corresponding field player would score a point and when three points were scored (according to the corresponding rules) that fielder would then have a turn at bat, and the prior batter would then take a field position. The batter's turn would be retired when any fielder had caught the predetermined number of fly balls to be "up" at bat. The first to bat was determined by the "choosing" ritual earlier described. No pitching to the batter was necessary as the batter would throw the ball up with one hand, at about shoulder height and bat the ball either after one bounce or before the ball hit ground. A stick ball bat and spaldeen were standard equipment for the game,

Another version of the game was played without any bat at all but was played using the vertical wall or side of a building. The made it easier to play the game during "recess" in the school yard. Rather than hitting the ball with a bat, the "batter" would stand near and facing the wall, with his back to the field players He would throw the ball against the wall such that the rebound from the wall would result in a "fly" ball over the field of play. The rules otherwise remained the same.

FLIES ARE UP

The side streets were at times relatively narrow as compared to a ball field. A typical side street was the width of one car lane plus two parking lanes on either side.

FOOTBALL (2 & 1 hand tag)

TYPE/CATEGORY: FOOTBALL

SETTING: SCHOOL YARD, PARK, FIELD/LOT, OR STREET

REQUIREMENTS: AT LEAST FOUR PLAYERS, A FOOTBALL

OBJECTIVE: TO SCORE THE MOST TOUCHDOWN POINTS

DESCRIPTION: The version of the game described below was played on the city streets. Typically two manhole covers about 100 feet apart and in the center of the street were the corresponding goals. The rules could also vary widely for street football depending on the street layout, width, location and number of parked cars, etc.. Alternate goal markers were parked cars, fire water hydrants, (the "pump"), parts of buildings, telephone/utility poles, etc. A minimum of four players divided into two teams was needed. Defensive and offensive team positions were determined through the choosing process. Because of the close distance between the goals, only four "downs" were permitted to make a goal. If the offensive team did not make the goal within four tries, the ball was then turned over to the other team. Blocking rather than tackling was common in street football. Rather the ball carrier was stopped by being tagged by any defensive player. The tag had to be either with one hand or two hands, as agreed to at the beginning of the game. The width of the street, distance between the goals and number of players were some of the considerations for deciding whether one or two hands were needed for a valid tag. Also and because of the narrow width of the playing area, the underhand lateral pass was very effective. Underhand forward passing (and backward passing, if agreed) was also permitted. Once out of the huddle the two teams would line up standing and, facing each other in parallel on the scrimmage line. The defensive player assigned to cover the offensive team quarterback, would "hike" the ball to the quarterback. Since he would be facing the quarterback in a standing position, the hike was simply a slight forward toss to the quarterback. Once the quarterback was in possession of the ball, the teams would be in motion. The offensive players would run and "jockey" for a clear and open receiving position. The quarterback was given a few seconds to seek out an open receiver before he could be rushed by the corresponding defensive player. The defensive player upon hiking the ball would count the remaining seconds out loud, for all to hear, and the quarterback would typically pass before or at the rush, occasionally attempting a run in the event that no open receiver was found. For example, upon hiking the ball, the count would be " one chimpanzee,..two chimpanzee,..three chimpanzee",...etc (or any other word that was felt to measure one second of time delay). If at the 10 second count (or other agreed to time delay) the ball had not been passed, the defensive player could then rush and tag the quarter back. During the 10 second count, the defensive players would cover the running receivers (you were either the quarterback or a receiver - there were no other offensive positions), to prevent a reception or intercept the pass. Rules also varied as to the quarterback's options during the count,..ie.. as to whether he could attempt a run during the count or only after the rush at the end of the count. If the ball was passed, the defensive player covering the quarterback could call out "pass" or "ball" to alert the other defensive players that the ball was in mid-flight. The 4th "down" was typically a " bomb" into the "end zone". Since the end zone did not need to have an outer boundary, the ball could be caught any distance beyond the manhole cover for a touch down. Failure to score a touchdown by the 4th down resulted in a conversion of offensive and defensive positions with the new offensive team taking possession at the location that either the ball was thrown from (for an incomplete pass) or the spot where either the quarterback or a receiver was tagged. After a touchdown, the teams would line up behind their corresponding goals and the ball was passed by the successful quarterback to the other team. Kicking to the other team was less common but when used it was typically a drop kick.

FOOTBALL 2 & 1 HAND TAG

Blocking rather than tackling was common in street football. Rather the ball carrier was stopped by being tagged by any defensive player. The tag had to be either with one hand or two hands, as agreed to at the beginning of the game. The width of the street, distance between the goals and number of players were some of the considerations for deciding whether one or two hands were needed for a valid tag.

HANDBALL

TYPE/CATEGORY: BALL GAME

SETTING: CITY PARK HANDBALL COURT OR SIDE OF A BUILDING

REQUIREMENTS: AT LEAST TWO PLAYERS, A SPALDEEN, AND SPECIAL GLOVE (FOR COLD WEATHER PLAYING)

OBJECTIVE: TO SCORE A GIVEN NUMBER OF POINTS BEFORE THE OTHER TEAM.

DESCRIPTION: The game was best played on a city park handball court. The handball courts in the city playgrounds included a concrete wall that may have measured about 20 or more feet in height and 25, or so, feet across. The wall was usually about 6 to 12 inches thick (depending on its overall height and size) and served two courts per wall, i.e. one court on each side of the wall. The courts were enclosed with tall chain link fencing. Boundary lines marking the fair ball playing area were painted both on the wall and the ground which was also concrete. The size of the playing area was approximately one half of a full tennis court. Earlier versions were played with an open hand. Later in the late sixties the use of a hand paddle began to emerge. However the rules were similar to paddle ball, squash and related wall rebound games. One team would serve the ball from the serving position which was normally at one side of the court (right side for a right hand server). The ball was served by hitting a spaldeen up against the wall. In serving , the player could first drop the ball near him and hit it on the first bounce. The ball would need to then hit the wall without a bounce. On the rebound of the first serve for some handball courts the ball had to bounce beyond a line that was drawn parallel and a few feet in front of the wall. After the serve rebound, the ball could rebound at any distance from the wall. Team players would alternately return and hit the ball back to the wall. The ball had to be hit within one bounce from the rebound. In cold weather days hitting the spaldeen with an open hand would cause a rather discomforting sting. Either well calloused palm and fingers (frequent and serious older players) or a thin leather glove with finger tips cut off , would mitigate the problem. Low fast and hard serves and ball returns were very effective. The serving team would continue to serve until it missed. The miss would result only in losing the serving position but no point would be scored against the team losing the serve. Points were scored for a team only when the non-serving team would miss. A typical game would last until 12 or 21 points were first scored by the winning team.

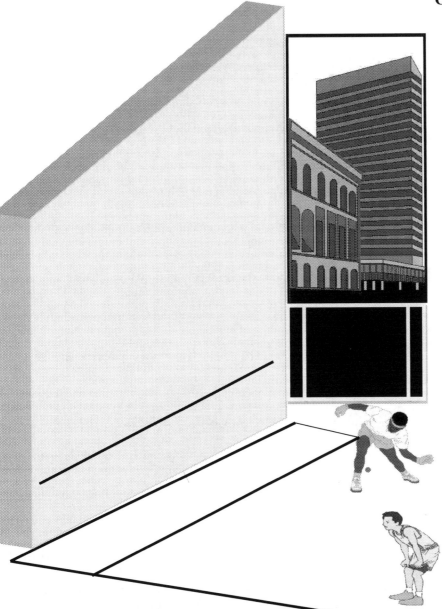

HANDBALL

The handball courts in the city playgrounds included a concrete wall that may have measured about 20 or more feet in height and 25, or so, feet across. The wall was usually about 6 to 12 inches thick (depending on its overall height and size) and served two courts per wall, i.e. one court on each side of the wall. The courts were enclosed with tall chain link fencing.

HEGGIES

TYPE/CATEGORY: RITUAL

SETTING: ANY WHERE WITHIN SIGHT OF A CANDY STORE

REQUIREMENTS: CANDY AND AT LEAST TWO PARTICIPANTS

OBJECTIVE: TO PLACE A CLAIM ON A SHARE OF SOMEONE'S CANDY.

DESCRIPTION: Though not a game, the practice was predominant and worth mention as part of the ritual of the inner city street pastimes. The idea of "heggies" was to place a claim on a share of someone's candy or similar goodies. The candy store like the ice cream parlor was very popular and frequently visited. The candy store was similar to the current day variety store. It offered a wide variety of individually wrapped and dispensed candies that could be bought in pieces and for pennies. Small toys, school supplies, and other odds and ends were also sold. Some candy stores offered fountain soda i.e. "egg creams", "cherry lime rickies", etc. Grocery stores in those days also included a candy section. Buying (and consuming) candy was very fulfilling and a measure of self reward and temporary status among peers due to limited pocket change that was better saved for the weekend movies. In addition to weekly allowances, the deposit   refund by returning soda bottles to the local store was another source of candy capital. The idea of the heggies ritual was to catch an unsuspecting purchaser of candy and require him or her to share with the other kids. Upon being approached by one or more other kids calling out the word "heggies" , the purchaser was required , by "common law" , to share the booty. However, if he or she was able to call out "fingers" before the "heggies" call, and hold up two wrapped fingers (index and third,..as in making a wish) ,..then the sharing was discretionary and not necessarily required. All edible items were fair game for the "heggies" ritual. Conceivably there would have been some kids that would have had the ritual down to a science, never purchasing candy throughout their entire youth and yet fulfilling their weekly requirements by preying on unsuspecting peers.

HEGGIES

Some candy stores offered fountain soda i.e. "egg creams", "cherry lime rickies", etc. Grocery stores in those days also included a candy section. Buying (and consuming) candy was very fulfilling and a measure of self reward and temporary status among peers due to limited pocket change that was better saved for the weekend movies.

HIDE AND SEEK

TYPE/CATEGORY: HIDING GAME

SETTING: CITY STREET, PLAYGROUND

REQUIREMENTS: AT LEAST THREE PLAYERS

OBJECTIVE: TO SEEK OUT HIDDEN PLAYERS

DESCRIPTION: This was the traditional hide and seek game. Through the choosing ritual one of the players became the seeker. The other players would hide. Playing hide and seek in the inner city provided many hiding places, i.e. behind cars, telephone poles, in hallways, behind stoops, garbage cans, in the nearby candy/grocery store. The rules would be established up front to determine what was out of bounds and not a hiding place. The seeker would close his/her eyes and stand facing a close wall or telephone pole which was known as the "base". Resting his head and forearm up against the wall or pole, the seeker would count out loud for all to hear (usually by "fives",i.e. 5, 10,15,20..etc). The number count was agreed to at the beginning, but would have to be long enough to permit players to find and settle into their hiding places The game required the seeker, upon discovering a hiding player, to run back and touch the base with a loud confirmation that a player had been discovered, i.e. "tap tap Charley, behind the black chevy". A common rule was that the first player to be caught became the seeker in the subsequent round. However if the discovered player could out run the seeker back to the base and tag the base first with an appropriate exclamation,..like "freeeee!!!", then such player would not be considered caught.. There were many places to hide and all with their corresponding advantages and drawbacks. For example, hiding in the hallway of an apartment building was risky , for most, because there was only one way out, i.e. through the front door and if the seeker was at the front door he or she would have the running advantage back to the base. However, if a player hiding in the hallway of a building saw the seeker approaching the hallway he could either make a dash out of the door and try to out run the seeker back to the base or sneak down the stairs at the back of the hallway which led either to the basement or the rear yard of the building, thus giving him alternative exits. Hiding behind cars, poles, trash cans, and in more open areas, would give the hiding player more open room to maneuver his way back to the base. Dropping down to look under cars could spot feet at a distance. The smart and obvious thing to do for players hiding behind cars was to jump up on a bumper and keep feet out of such view. Once the last player was caught the game would begin over with a new seeker (the first player caught), unless the seeker was unsuccessful in discovering any of the players. The objective of most players was to continue to hide and not be caught or be the first caught in the round. Good hiding places were rarely shared if they could be kept a secret. If a player was able to make a break for the base from a real good hiding spot while the seeker was off in another direction, the player's hiding spot was not disclosed and could be kept a secret for future use again. Speed and clever hiding spots were advantages to the game.

HIDE AND SEEK

However, if a player hiding in the hallway of a building saw the seeker approaching the hallway he could either make a dash out of the door and try to out run the seeker back to the base or sneak down the stairs at the back of the hallway which led either to the basement or the rear yard of the building,

JACKS

TYPE/CATEGORY: BALL BOUNCING GAME

SETTING: ANY INDOOR OR OUTDOOR LOCATION SUCH AS A HALL WAY WHERE ONE COULD SIT ON A SMOOTH FLOOR SURFACE.

REQUIREMENTS: TWO OR MORE PLAYERS, A SET OF 12 "JACKS" AND A SMALL RUBBER BALL.

OBJECTIVE: TO BE THE FIRST TO COMPLETE ALL SUCCESSFUL ROUNDS AS DESCRIBED.

DESCRIPTION: The ball used in the game of jacks was a small rubber ball about the size of a quarter in diameter. The jacks were small metal objects that resembled a three dimensional star with six spokes and with a diameter of about a nickel coin. The tips of 4 of the spokes were rounded while the two in-line spokes, considered the vertical axis, were pointed. This game was an extremely entertaining and at times frustrating game which required dexterity, and excellent coordination of eye and hand motion. The players would sit on the smooth floor surface and take turns at the play which went as follows. The first player holding the 12 jacks in one hand would cast them on the floor within reach but hoping that the jacks fell individually spaced. A problem could arise if two jacks landed touching or interlocked. With the jacks spread in front of the player and within reach, the player would then throw the small rubber ball up in the air with one hand and at about eye level. In the second or two that it took for the ball to bounce once and be caught with the same hand, the player would need to scoop up one jack piece with that same hand, i.e. between the throw of the ball and catching the ball on one bounce. After scooping up the first jack, the player would again throw up the ball and attempt to catch the second jack, and then a third throw for the third jack and so on until all 12 jacks had been individually scooped in turn. If jacks fell interlocked or touching each other, such could result in a lost turn because, during the scoop, no other jack could be moved or touched. Only the target jack being scooped could be moved. Missing the jack on the scoop, which was more of a sweeping quick grab by the hand, or moving/touching another jack during the scooping motion, or missing the ball or failing to catch it on the first bounce after a successful scoop would lose the player's turn. That player would need to begin from the first jack on his/her next turn until the all 12 jacks had been scooped. This would complete the "onezies" round. Simple as it sounds there was a lot of chance for error and completing the "onezies" round was not as simple. But the real challenge began with the "twozies" round. A successful completion of the "onezies" lead to the "twozies" in which case two jacks had to be scooped at a time, i.e. after casting the jacks, the player would need to scoop two jacks at a time between the throw and the catch on one bounce. Successful scooping of all the 12 jacks by pairs (six successful and consecutive scoops of 2 jacks at a time) would then lead to the "threezies" , "fourzees", "fivezees", and so on. Players would lose their turn if they faulted in any round, but a successfully completed round would not have to be repeated on the subsequent turn. Each player would advance to their next round and once a player reached and successfully completed the "twelvezies" round, he or she would then reverse the process and play the rounds in reverse, i.e. "elevenzies" to "tenzies" to "ninezies" etc. The winning player would be the first to complete "onezies" on the reverse try or 23 rounds in total. Nerves of steel, patience, dexterity, quick eye/hand coordination were all key to winning.

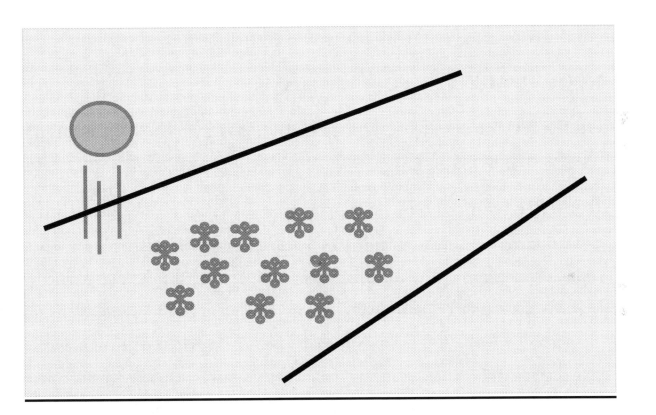

JACKS

Missing the jack on the scoop, which was more of a sweeping quick grab by the hand, or moving/touching another jack during the scooping motion, or missing the ball or failing to catch it on the first bounce after a successful scoop would lose the player's turn................ Nerves of steel, patience, dexterity, quick eye/hand coordination were all key to winning.

THE OFFICIAL COMPENDIUM OF INNER CITY STREET GAMES

JOHNNY ON THE PONY

TYPE/CATEGORY: CONTACT GAME

SETTING: CITY STREET, SIDEWALK , A BUILDING WALL

REQUIREMENTS: ABOUT TEN PLAYERS

OBJECTIVE: TO MAINTAIN THE JUMPING (OFFENSIVE) POSITION AS LONG AS POSSIBLE

DESCRIPTION: Johnny on the pony was a contact pastime that relied on gravity, strength and player agility. Two teams of five players per team was an optimal arrangement. The offensive team position was the desired position in that the team members, individually, and from a running start, would leap on to the defensive team. The defensive team would be positioned as an elongated pony or horse. To form the pony, the defensive team members would arrange themselves as follows: the first defensive team member (typically the weakest) would stand with his back up against a building wall and act as a cushion for the defensive team "pony". A chubby gut also qualified for this position. The next team member, facing the "cushion man" , would bend at the waist and nest his head and shoulders in a safe and comfortable position around the cushion man's mid section (as if in a tackle position) the next team member standing behind and also facing the wall, would bend at the waist and somewhat overlap the first bending player. Each subsequent player, in line, would bend at the waist and support his upper body on the prior bent player. In this arrangement the defensive team would form an elongated pony - with the cushion man standing at the head of the pony and the remaining four or so players bending at the waist and supporting themselves in line as above described. The offensive team would stand at a distance of about fifty feet or so. In turn each offensive team member would run and leap on to the man-made pony and hold his position. The leap was similar to how the western cowboy heroes in the movies would run and mount their horses from the rear. The objective of the first player was to leap as far up and front on to the pony as possible to accommodate and leave room for the remaining players. Once on the pony the player would lean down and rest his upper body on the pony because remaining players would probably land on the earlier jumpers. Inching up towards the cushion man after landing was not permitted. The landed position had to be maintained. The last to leap the pony was normally the lightest and highest jumping player, because by the time his turn came (and if the prior players were able to hold their positions on the pony) this last player would be looking at a mound of about four players saddled on top of the pony holding on for dear life. If the first jumpers were not successful in their leaps in leaving adequate space, the remaining players could fail to land in a stable position (holding a leap on top of two or more players near the rear of the pony was very difficult). The jumping team would also lose their offensive position if any jumper made an unsuccessful leap or fell from the saddle while waiting for the reaming players to jump. Once the offensive team was successful in having all team members mount the pony, and if the pony team players were able to support the jumpers for a count of about ten seconds, then the teams would trade positions for another round, with the prior jumpers then forming a pony. The offensive players would attempt to collapse the pony during their jumps by jumping high and trying to pile as many jumpers as possible to weaken the pony. If they broke the pony then they would continue as the jumping team for another turn. It's no wonder we suffer so many back problems today.

JOHNNY ON THE PONY

Once the offensive team was successful in having all team members mount the pony, and if the pony team players were able to support the jumpers for a count of about ten seconds, then the teams would trade positions for another round, with the prior jumpers then forming a pony. The offensive players would attempt to collapse the pony during their jumps by jumping high and trying to pile as many jumpers as possible to weaken the pony.

JUMP ROPE

TYPE/CATEGORY: JUMPING GAME

SETTING: CITY STREET, SIDEWALK

REQUIREMENTS: FOR SINGLE ROPE JUMPING - ONE PLAYER, A MINIMUM OF FOUR WHEN GROUP JUMPING. A CLOTHES LINE OR SIMILAR ROPE

OBJECTIVE: TO MAINTAIN YOUR TURN IN JUMPING WITHOUT STEPPING OR TRIPPING ON THE ROPE

DESCRIPTION: The individual rope jumping was similar to the exercise that boxers and other athletes use. The group game was typically played with a minimum of four players and usually by the girls in the neighborhood. The more common jump rope games were single handed rope and "double dutch", and in the single rope jump a rope about the thickness of a clothes line (used for hanging laundry to air dry) was used. A rope was extended at about ten to fifteen feet between two players, each holding one end of the rope. With arms lowered the rope would touch the ground at the suspended midpoint between the two end players. The end players' ("enders") job was to turn the rope to allow one or more players in the center (between the turning players) to jump the rope as it passed under the jumpers feet. The jumpers would jump to various rhymes or songs such as "Fire fire false alarm, Mary fell into her boyfriend's arm's , how many kisses did she receive",...at this point in the rhyme, the player, Mary, would continue jumping but with her eyes closed and the other players would count how many times she would jump with closed eyes before faulting, or stepping on the rope. With more players another version was called " J space ". For this game a group of jumpers would position themselves in single file with the first jumper adjacent to one of the enders. Then in turn each player would   follow the previous jumper for one jump. Since the rope was continuously turning they would have to carefully time their entry into the jump area , jump only for one rope turn and then quickly move out before being caught by the turning rope. It was also a rhythmic pace such as " A space and a monkey's face"...while the rope continued turning , the jumper would enter the jump area, jump on the words "a space" move out on the balance of the phrase and to the back of the line. The next jumper would move in on " B space " etc. Upon faulting the jumper would replace an ender and the ender would join the line of jumpers. Of the more challenging version was the "double dutch" jump. In this game two ropes would be turned by the enders, i.e. the ends of on rope held in the right hand of one ender and in the left hand of the other. Their other hands would hold the second rope. Facing each other the enders would hold the two ropes in parallel and again allowing the midpoints of the rope to touch the ground when their arms were dropped. The two ropes were then turned alternately and inwardly but continuously turning. The challenge was to enter the jump area and repeatedly jump the two ropes which would pass under the jumpers' feet and over their heads from opposite directions. This version required excellent timing, skill and agility and was a very entertaining "spectator's sport" for the neighborhood boys.

JUMP ROPE

The jumpers would jump to various rhymes or songs such as "Fire fire false alarm, Mary fell into her boyfriend's arm's , how many kisses did she receive",..

KICK THE CAN

TYPE/CATEGORY: HIDING GAME

SETTING: CITY STREET - PLAY GROUND, VACANT LOTS

REQUIREMENTS: THREE OR MORE PLAYERS AND A TIN CAN

OBJECTIVE: THE CAN KICKER'S OBJECTIVE WAS TO SEEK AND CAPTURE THE REMAINING PLAYERS

DESCRIPTION: The game was played after a choosing/elimination process, where one player became the can kicker. The other players would stand in-line (as in a scrimmage line) and upon the can being kicked, players would run and hide. The Kicker would return the can on the ground to "home base" and then proceed to seek out the other players and attempt to capture them. Upon finding a player, the kicker would then race back to where the can had been placed (home base) and exclaim "1,2,3 kick the can I found so and so behind the telephone pole,..etc.". However, any remaining uncaught player could attempt to rescue capture players by running into home base and kicking the can out of the area and exclaiming "freeeeee". However if caught in the act by the can kicker, the player attempting the rescue would be it. If all players were caught by the kicker, then the first player to have been caught would be it.

> ### *KICK THE CAN*
> The Kicker would return the can on the ground to "home base" and then proceed to seek out the other players and attempt to capture them.

KILLER (ACEY DEUCY OR SCULLY)

TYPE/CATEGORY: BOTTLE CAP FLOOR GAME

SETTING: CITY STREET - SIDEWALK AREA OR STREET.

REQUIREMENTS: A MINIMUM OF TWO PLAYERS, CHALK, BOTTLE CAPS

OBJECTIVE: TO BE THE FIRST PLAYER TO SAFELY "SHOOT" HIS BOTTLE CAP SEQUENTIALLY INTO THE NUMBERED BOXES.

DESCRIPTION: The game was a challenge and exciting. Chalk was needed to draw the "game board" on the ground of either a sidewalk or street. The playing area was a rather intricate array of numbered boxes which were arranged along the perimeter of an imaginary rectangle with the final cluster of numbered boxes in the center. The play area (rectangle) typically measured about ten feet by fifteen feet. Two adjoining square boxes about five inches on side were drawn at each corner and numbered in diagonal sequence, i.e. the two boxes at the northeast corner were numbered 1 and 3 while the south west corner boxes were numbered 2 and 4. The northwest boxes were numbered 5 and 7 and the southeast boxes 6 and 8. Then midway along the imaginary two longer side lines of the rectangle (assume the long sides of the rectangle ran east to west on top and west to east on bottom) , then two more adjoining square boxes were drawn at the top and numbered 9 and 11 and at the opposite bottom of the rectangle two more boxes were numbered 10 and 12. In the center of the playing area either an "ace deucy" rectangle or circle was drawn about two feet in diameter with a small three or four inch diameter circle in the middle. From that center small circle lines were drawn to the edges of the larger acey deucy circle or rectangle similar to pie slices. The lines divided the "pie" or rectangle into about 5 equal slices or sections. The players would establish the rules for entering their bottle caps into the play area. With one cap per player the players would "shoot" their caps on the ground. The caps could not be lifted from the ground but would have to be slid with a flick of the fingers. The typical finger flick or shot was a quick jerky release of the middle finger which would be held down by the thumb with pressure prior to the release. The hand was held close to the ground with the releasing finger parallel to the ground. A good effective shot could send the bottle cap clear across the diagonal of the play area or about 20 feet. The idea was to shoot into each of the numbered boxes in sequence. The cap would need to slide and stop clear in the box and not stop touching any of the box lines. A common tactic that served two purposes was to hit another player's cap with your shot. By hitting another player's cap, the other player was knocked out of his path and would automatically win the shooting player, entry into his next box goal. A sharp shooter would obtain entry into the boxes primarily by hitting other players' caps on his shots. Some players would fill the empty center of their caps with gum or wax to give it more weight and momentum on the asphalt or concrete ground. Going from numbered box to box, if a player did not make entry in one shot he would need to wait his next turn to continue attempting entry into the numbered boxes in sequence. Upon entering a numbered box the player would take another shot at the next box. In shooting the player would either aim for his next numbered box or hit another player's cap to gain automatic entry into the next box. Once all twelve boxes were entered the most difficult shooting was at the acey deucy center box. The acey deucy box would need to be entered into one of the "pie slices" then in the same turn the player would need to enter each adjoining pie section and finally into the center most small circle. During the turn , if the player's cap landed on one of the section's line and did not clear, the player would need to wait till his next turn and enter all sections around the small center circle. Entering the sections   and then the small center circle by clearing all the lines in one turn resulted in a win. This last part was the most frustrating stage of the game, because it could take multiple turns to achieve this and in the mean time the trailing players would have time to catch up. If they did , the crowded center " acey deucy" box made winning much more difficult. Real die hards would reverse the play upon winning and replay the game with the boxes played in descending order.

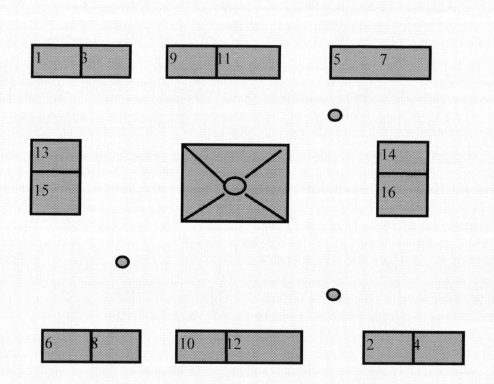

KILLER-ACEY DEUCY

Upon entering a numbered box the player would take another shot at the next box. In shooting the player would either aim for his next numbered box or hit another player's cap to gain automatic entry into the next box. ....The last part was the most frustrating stage of the game, because it could take multiple turns to achieve and in the mean time the trailing players would have time to catch up.

KING OF THE HILL

TYPE/CATEGORY: BODY CONTACT

SETTING: ANY LOT OR AREA THAT OFFERED A SMALL MOUND

REQUIREMENTS: A GROUP OF THREE OR MORE PLAYERS

OBJECTIVE: TO REMAIN ON TOP OF THE MOUND

DESCRIPTION: The game was a simple free for all wrestling match among all the players. A mound of dirt, grass, or rock in an open lot or similar setting was charged by the players. On the way up and upon reaching the "summit" the players would wrestle and attempt to dismount each other from the top of the mound or hill. The hill would need to be large enough to accommodate the players. In the winter time the game was played on top of the large snow mounds that were created by the city snow removal trucks when clearing the streets after a snow storm.

KING OF THE HILL

On the way up and upon reaching the "summit" the players would wrestle and attempt to dismount each other from the top of the mound or hill.

MARBLES

TYPE/CATEGORY: MARBLE SHOOTING GAME

SETTING: CITY STREETS

REQUIREMENTS: TWO OR MORE PLAYERS, CHALK, SHOE BOX, BAG OF MARBLES

OBJECTIVE: TO WIN AS MANY OF AN OPPONENT'S MARBLES AS POSSIBLE

DESCRIPTION: There were many versions of marbles. In one version, a circle was drawn with chalk on the street of about two feet in diameter. A diameter line was drawn within the circle. Then each player would contribute one, two or as many marbles as agreed. The contributed marbles were then placed in line on the diameter line. From another shooting line positioned parallel to the diameter line but about five to ten feet away , the players would take turns and shoot at the marbles in the circle. An imaginary line connecting the centers of the circle diameter line and the shooting line would fall perpendicular to the two lines. The marbles were shot with the flick of either the middle finger as described in the "killer- Acey Deucy" game or with the thumb. If a shooter's marble landed in the circle it would remain there as fair game and added to the pot of potential winnings. The idea was to shoot as many of your own and the opponent's marbles out of the circle including the shooter's marble. The shooter would win and keep any marbles that in turn he shot out of the circle. The starting or shooting line above described was used only for the beginning shot. All other shots were taken from the position that a player's marble came to rest in the prior turn. Players would shoot in turn. A player could also win an opponent's shooting marble that was in the play area but not in the circle by hitting it during his turn. The game was played until all of the marbles were shot out of the circle and then another "set up" of marbles in the circle could be made. If a player lost his shooting marble by being hit by an opponent, he would need to go back to the shooting line and play a new marble. Another version of the game was played with a shoe box. Small openings would be cut into the edge of one longer side of a shoe box. When placed open side down on the ground and up against a wall the small openings would become ground level targets. The players would take turns shooting marbles to see how many they could get into the shoe box. In all the various versions of marbles the intent was to win points or marbles either by shooting them at other marbles or at targets. The common marble was about the size of a nickel in diameter. Larger marbles , about the size of a quarter, could also be used. Players took precaution not to risk playing with their "beauties" as some of the marbles had very intricate and colorful designs. The more beat up and dull marbles were used in the games that offered a risk of losing the marbles.

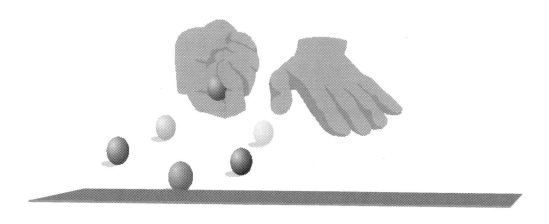

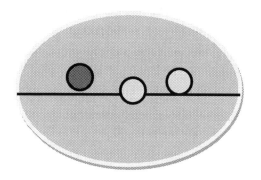

MARBLE SHOOTING GAME

From another shooting line positioned parallel to the diameter line but about
five to ten feet away , the players would take turns and shoot at the marbles
in the circle.

MOTHER MAY I

TYPE/CATEGORY: GROUP PLAY

SETTING: SIDEWALK OR PLAY GROUND

REQUIREMENTS: A MINIMUM OF THREE PLAYERS

OBJECTIVE: TO BE THE FIRST TO REACH THE FRONT OF THE PLAY AREA.

DESCRIPTION: This game was rather simple. One leader was chosen to make the call as to whether players could move or not. The leader would be positioned about fifty to one hundred feet away from the group of players. The players would stand abreast and in line at the far end of the play area facing the leader. In turn each player would ask out loud "Mother may I take a giant step",..or " small step",...or "three small steps" , etc. . The leader would then reply by "yes you may" or "no you may not" . The leader could offer an alternative after declining the request such as "you may take two steps and one giant step" or the player could make another request in any combination of giant and regular steps. The trick to this game was recalling to request and confirm the leader's acceptance prior to moving. The following example leader and player dialogue may illustrate the play: player would request "Mother may I take two giant steps" , leader would respond "no you may not" , player then could request "mother may I take three steps" , leader responds "no you may not, you may take one giant step". At this point if the player were to make a move without again simply saying "may I" and waiting for the leader to finally respond "yes you may" , then the player would be sent back to the starting line. Playing this game was really a play on words along the lines of the Simon Says game. A good leader could cause enough confusion and anxiety in this slow paced "race" such that the final reconfirmation could be easily forgotten causing players to be sent back to the starting line. The player to first reach the leader was the winning player to then become leader on the next round. A major frustration in this game was to be sent to the starting line after moving well along the way to the finish. This would further frustrate the players, increasing their anxiety and further increasing their likelihood for further error. The game was enjoyable on cool summer evenings.

 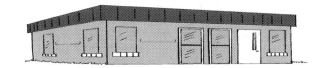

MOTHER MAY I
The player to first reach the leader was the winning player to then become leader on the next round. A major frustration in this game was to be sent to the starting line after moving well along the way to the finish.

NOK HOCKEY

TYPE/CATEGORY: AN ACTION BOARD GAME

SETTING: AT THE PLAYGROUND

REQUIREMENTS: A NOK HOCKEY TABLE PROVIDED BY THE CITY PLAYGROUND

OBJECTIVE: TO OUTSCORE THE OPPOSING PLAYER AND TWO PLAYERS

DESCRIPTION: The nok hockey game was a board game played with a round wooden "hockey" puck about the size of a silver dollar. The board was rectangular and measured about two feet by three to four feet. The opposing players would stand at the opposite ends of the board facing each other and in front of the short sides. The board was typically placed on a stand or table at about waist height. At the edges of the board was a one to two inch wood trim to keep the wooden puck in play and for rebound shots. The goal at each end of the board was a small slot cut into the center of the wood trim edge directly in front of each player. The slot was about three times the puck's diameter in width and about two to three times the puck's thickness in height. The players each wood use a small wooden "L" shaped stick about ten inches long to shoot the wooden puck. The idea was to score goal points by getting the puck through the opposing goal slot. Straight shots were not possible because a small 3 inch square block was positioned about 6 inches in front of each goal slot. As a result most goals would need to be scored by rebounding the puck off the sides. Conceptually, the idea was similar to angle shooting required in many billiard (pool) games. The players would start by dropping the puck in the center of the table and vie for the first shot as in regular ice hockey. After the first shot the players would alternate shots. Each player would shoot the puck from the position that it came to rest after the opponent's shot. Though most shots were rebounds, an occasional diagonal shot was possible if the puck came to rest in a position that would permit a clear and direct shot passed the square goal tending block. The position for such a clear shot was typically close to the edge of the board and within the opponent's half of the board. The players were not permitted to goal tend and could only rely on the small wooden block in front of their slotted goal to block an opponent's shot. A good eye for angle and rebound shots was an advantage. There were many rebound combinations particularly using the inside corners of the edge trim. At these inside corners a small piece of wood was put at an angle across and in front of the inside corner forming a small triangle at the corners. A shot made along side and parallel to the long edge of the board and into the inside corner at the end of that edge would rebound the puck at about 90 degrees. On occasion, it would hit the angled side of the goal block and rebound at another 90 degrees and into the slotted goal with luck and skill. Winning a goal permitted the player to place the puck anywhere on his half of the table. Sometimes this would allow the player to make continuous goals, if he had a favorite angle shot. The winning player would continue to play with another challenger until losing a game.

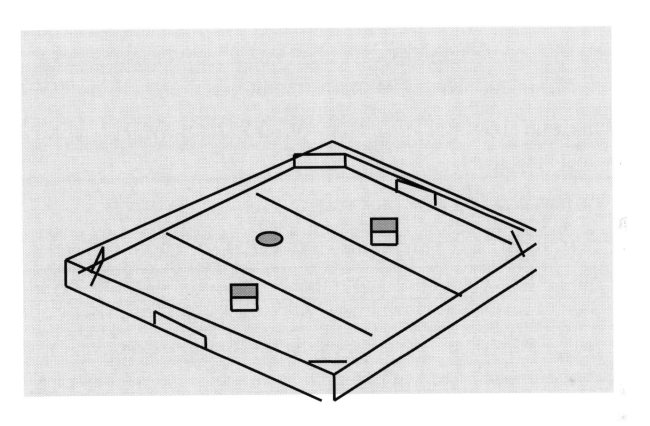

NOK HOCKEY

The players were not permitted to goal tend and could only rely on the small wooden block in front of their slotted goal to block an opponent's shot. A good eye for angle and rebound shots was an advantage.

PEA SHOOTERS

TYPE/CATEGORY: SEASONAL ACTIVITY

SETTING: ANY WHERE AROUND THE "BLOCK"

REQUIREMENTS: PLASTIC TUBE (OR SIPPING STRAW) AND A BAG OF DRIED PEAS

OBJECTIVE: TO HIT TARGETS WITH PEAS

DESCRIPTION: This pastime was seasonal to the extent that it was not played throughout the year. Though it would not necessarily occur at the same time each year. It would become popular only about once per year and when the local candy store would get in a new supply of the pea shooters. The pea shooters were small plastic tubes just a bit larger in diameter and length than a sipping straw. Kids would purchase a small paper bag of dried peas, about half a pound. The shooters were used like a "blow gun" in that the peas were shot from the mouth through the tubes by blowing. The peas would go far and could easily cover 100 to 200 feet if the kid had a healthy pair of lungs. The activity was risky and could end up hurting players if care was not used as at times the players would target each other and chase each other with the shooters. This pastime lent itself to mischief. The weapon could be easily and quickly concealed as the pea hit its unsuspecting target.

PEA SHOOTERS

The pea shooters were small plastic tubes just a bit larger in diameter and length than a sipping straw.

PITCHING PENNIES

TYPE/CATEGORY: PASTIME

SETTING: SIDEWALK NEAR A WALL

REQUIREMENTS: TWO OR MORE PLAYERS

OBJECTIVE: TO WIN AN OPPONENT'S COINS

DESCRIPTION: This pastime was played on the sidewalks facing a building wall. The idea was to pitch coins underhand to see how close to the bottom of the vertical wall the coin would land. Players would stand at the curb end of a sidewalk and pitch the coins toward the base of the wall. Coins would all be of the same denomination. The tossed coin that landed closest to the wall would win all the other coins tossed. Landing a coin on top of another player's coin would negate the under coin's position. For example , the only way to beat a coin that had landed up against and touching the wall was to land on top of it. Coins had to be tossed in such a way to avoid bouncing away from the base of the wall or to avoid rolling away. One method was to toss the coin such that it would have a forward flipping action with the intent of continuing to flip forward and toward the wall when landing. In this case the coin was tossed with a skipping action to land before the wall with the intent that the continuing forward flipping on the ground would bring it closer to the wall. Another technique was to pitch the coin without causing it to flip in mid air but with the leading edge sloped downward. The idea with this technique was for the coin to drop sharply near the wall and "bite" the ground where it landed. In this case, the coin was tossed in an arching trajectory to land as close to the wall as possible.

PITCHING PENNIES

Landing a coin on top of another player's coin would negate the under coin's position. For example , the only way to beat a coin that had landed up against and touching the wall was to land on top of it.

POPSICLE STICK BOUNCE

TYPE/CATEGORY: BOUNCING BALL GAME

SETTING: SIDEWALK

REQUIREMENTS: TWO PLAYERS, ICE CREAM POP STICK, SPALDEEN

OBJECTIVE: TO OUTSCORE YOUR OPPONENT

DESCRIPTION: This game was real simple. Two players got together with a "spaldeen" and an ice cream pop (or popsicle) stick. The popsicle stick was placed on the line which was coincident to two concrete squares of the sidewalk. Each player would stand at the outer line of either one of the two adjoining sidewalk squares. The popsicle stick was the flat wooden ice cream stick that was the handle for ice cream "pops". They were about the length of a pencil and not much wider than such. Popsicles were ice cream bars on a stick. As an alternative a pencil or small twig would serve the purpose. Of course, there was choosing as to which player would be first.. The object was to hit the popsicle stick with a toss of the ball. The ball was tossed at the stick which was on the ground and midway between the two players with the intent to bounce it on the stick. The opposing player would catch the ball on the one bounce and then toss the spaldeen back also with a bounce and the same intent. Hitting the stick with the ball scored a point. The winner was the first to score a predetermined number of points. If the stick slid toward and closer to either player when hit with the ball, this resulted in a disadvantage to the furthest player and an obvious advantage to the closest player. Because of this , under some rules, the stick was repositioned in the middle after a score. An old popsicle stick would stay in place better than a new one which would go flying at times. A good eye and coordination was the requirement. This game would be played when there wasn't too much of anything else happening or while waiting for the rest of the group to come together.

POPSICLE STICK BOUNCE

If the stick slid toward and closer to either player when hit with the ball, this resulted in a disadvantage to the furthest player and an obvious advantage to the closest player. Because of this , under some rules, the stick was repositioned in the middle after a score.

POTSY (HOP SCOTCH)

TYPE/CATEGORY: BODY BALANCING PASTIME

SETTING: CITY PARK , SCHOOL YARD PLAYGROUND, OR SIDE WALK

REQUIREMENTS: TWO OR MORE PLAYERS, CHALK

OBJECTIVE: TO BE THE FIRST TO COMPLETE THE BOARD OBSTACLE
COURSE

DESCRIPTION: This game was a mini obstacle course which required hopping on
one leg in and out of an array of boxes that were drawn with chalk on the ground.
The overall play area measured about four feet wide by about ten feet long. The
game was played primarily by the girls on the block. The player would begin at the
base of the play area which was an array of chalk-drawn boxes as follows. Two
adjoining squares about 1 to 2 feet wide were drawn at the base of the array and
numbered 1 & 2. On top of these two boxes a third similar sized box was drawn but
located with its center directly over the line dividing the two lower boxes. The box
was numbered 3. Then two more adjoining boxes were drawn on top of the number
three box with the line dividing the two boxes aligned with the center of the lower
number 3 box. The pattern of alternating single and double boxes was continued
until about eight boxes were drawn and numbered. At the end or top of the box
array a resting box was drawn the width of two adjoining boxes. The player would
start at the base and drop a small item such as a hair pin in the number 1 box. The
player would then on one leg hop in sequence up the remaining boxes. At no time
could she place more than one foot in a box and stepping on a line or falling or
losing her balance would result in a fault and she would lose her turn. If the player

made the round trip successfully, i.e., up and back on the return trip down the boxes, the player would need to stop at the box preceding the box containing the dropped item. Still balancing on one leg, she had to bend down to pick up the item only with one hand and then hop over that box and out of the lowest box back to the bottom of the array. Having completed her "onezee's" she would then proceed to her "twozee's" by dropping the item into the number two box. She then would hop into the 1 box, skip over the 2 box (containing the item) and attempt another round trip. On the return trip, she would stop on one leg in the number 3 box, just before the number 2 box to pick up the item. The game became more difficult as the target box into which the item was to be thrown became farther away from the base line. If the player missed that target box or the item landed on a line of the box (it had to land clear of all lines inside the box) the turn was lost. The resting box at the top of the array was the turning point and permitted the player to step into it with both feet for a short rest before making the return trip back down the array. Once a player successfully completed her "eightzee's" (depending on the number of boxes) she would throw her item into any box and claim ownership to that box. With chalk her name was placed in the box and for the remainder of the game the other players could not use that box in their play of the game. This could make it more of an obstacle for other players, because when dropping their item into an adjoining box, the other players would need to pass over two boxes. Which was not a very easy hop on one leg. The player who owned one or more boxes would be the only one allowed to step in the boxes and could do so with both feet to either rest or pick up the their item.

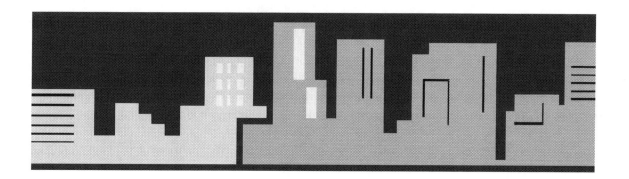

POTSY (HOP SCOTCH)

The player who owned one or more boxes would be the only one allowed

to step in the boxes……….

RED LIGHT GREEN LIGHT

TYPE/CATEGORY: GROUP LEADER GAME

SETTING: CITY SIDEWALK OR PLAYGROUND

REQUIREMENTS: MINIMUM THREE PLAYERS

OBJECTIVE: TO BE THE FIRST PLAYER TO REACH A GOAL LINE

DESCRIPTION: One player would be chosen to be the leader or "caller". The leader would stand with his back to and about fifty to one hundred feet from the players. The players would line up abreast as in the "Mother may I" game at about arms length apart on each side. The leader would then call out the phrase "red light green light one, two, three" and then quickly turn his head to look at the players. The players would only be permitted to move forward towards the leader during the call and as long as their movement was not caught or seen by the caller. They would move forward in short jumps or skip and at times take a leap or two, but the idea was to not be caught in action when the caller turned his head. If the caller saw any player's movement, even if a player had just come to a stop from a jump or leap but was caught moving to maintain his balance, the player would need to go back to the starting line. The caller could attempt to trick the players by turning around more than once before starting the call. The caller could also stump the players and force a fault by not completing the phrase and turning unexpectedly. The trick for the players was to decide when to creep with little, few or no steps and when to lunge forward on a leap and avoid being caught in the action. The leader/caller stood on the goal line and the first player to come within reach and tag the caller would win. The game was exciting but also very frustrating for players caught in action and sent back to the starting line. Being sent back and therefore falling behind the other players would make players attempt to catch up with faster, longer and more frequent leaps which further increased the likelihood of being caught and again sent to the starting line. The typical winning player would be the one who best timed the larger moves and reduced the risk of faulting by moving slower as he neared the goal line.

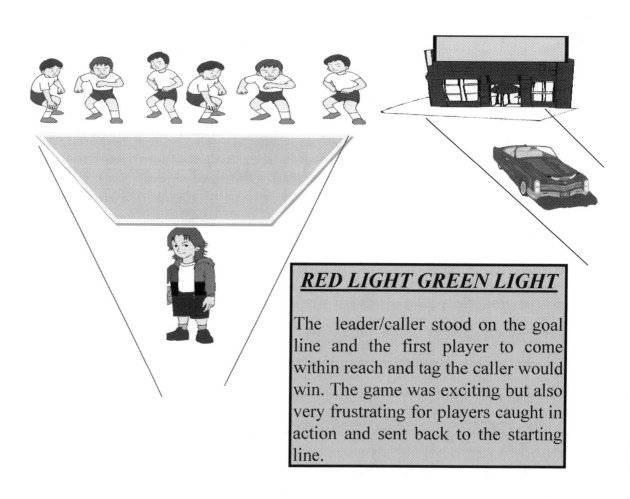

RED LIGHT GREEN LIGHT

The leader/caller stood on the goal line and the first player to come within reach and tag the caller would win. The game was exciting but also very frustrating for players caught in action and sent back to the starting line.

RINGOLEVIO

TYPE/CATEGORY: TEAM TAG

SETTING: CITY STREETS, BUILDINGS

REQUIREMENTS: CHALK TO MARK THE CAPTIVE ZONE

OBJECTIVE: TO CAPTURE ALL THE MEMBERS OF THE OPPOSING TEAM.

DESCRIPTION: The game was an exciting and fast paced combination of tag and hide and seek. It was played between two teams of a minimum of 3 players per team. After the two team members were established and team captains chosen, the captains would choose to determine which team would become the free team that had to be chased and captured by the remaining pursuing team. At a mutually agreed location and on the ground a rectangular box measuring about ten feet by fifteen feet was drawn with chalk from the base of a vertical wall or side of a building. The box served as the holding area for captured members of the free team. The pursuing team would seek out and chase members of the free team and the capture required holding or tackling the team member long enough to call out "ringaleevio 1,2,3, ringaleevio 1,2,3, ringaleevio 1,2,3," alternative/added phrases also were used such as "ringaleevio coca cola 1,2,3".....etc. Once captured the team member would have to stay in the prisoner's box. With at least one prisoner captured, it was typical for the pursuing team to keep at least one player guarding the box. The reason for this was that prisoners could be freed simply by another uncaptured team member running into the box just for enough time to call out the word "free". Even if the freeing team member was captured by the guard or another pursuing player, as long as he was able to place his foot in the box and yell out "free" during his capture and before his capture was complete, then all other captured players were automatically released and became free to run away. It was not uncommon for a team member to sacrifice himself in an attempt to free the box particularly if many prisoners had already been captured. Guarding the box was tricky because more than one of the free team members could simultaneously attempt to free the prisoners. An attempt from multiple sides could not be defended effectively with only one or two guards. So as the prison count grew more guards would need to be added and this would reduce the number of pursuing runners or chasers. The guards could stay close to the box but guarding too close to the box was also a risk if it gave the opportunity for the freeing team player to step in during his capture and free the others. Various strategies could be used. For example, at the outset of the game the faster runners of the chasing team could chase and capture the slower runners of the free team, and the slower chasers would gradually become box guards as the number of prisoners grew. Once all the free team members were captured, then the roles would be reversed between the teams. Depending on the speed of the chasers compared to the remaining free players, the chasing team could double up or "double team" the free players. But the corresponding risk was the reduced protection of the prisoner's box. Rules had to be set as to what places were and were not out of bounds for running and hiding. As one example, the teams could agree that running into the hall of a building was permitted only if the same entrance was used to exit the building (most apartment buildings had additional first floor hall exits down to the basements or back yards that lead out to the sides and back). There were many obstacles that served either team in the chase. Parked cars made the chase more difficult and in some cases the parked cars could conceal a sneak attack by one or more players looking to free its prison team members. A most frustrating event for the pursuing team was to have most prisoners freed by an unsuspecting player surfacing out of nowhere, while other free players were being chased. In some neighborhoods the name was phonetically pronounced "ringoleevio".

RINGOLEVIO

Depending on the speed of the chasers compared to the remaining free players, the chasing team could double up or "double team" the free players. But the corresponding risk was the reduced protection of the prisoner's box. Rules had to be set as to what places were and were not out of bounds for running and hiding.

SALUGEE

TYPE/CATEGORY: A FORM OF CATCH

SETTING: ANY WHERE

REQUIREMENTS: AT LEAST THREE PLAYERS AND AN ITEM
BELONGING TO ONE

OBJECTIVE: THE GAME WAS A FORM OF TEASING

DESCRIPTION: Salugee was a form of hazing or teasing an unsuspecting
and unwilling player. An article (hat, book, ball, toy, etc) was passed or tossed
among the kids and the owner of the article would try to reclaim the item that
had been taken from him or her. The "game" was very impromptu. If an item was
taken from one of the kids, the minute the word "salugee" was heard , all the
kids (except the property owner) would join in this game of catch.

SALUGEE

If an item was taken from one of the kids, the minute the word "salugee"
was heard , all the kids (except the property owner) would join in this
game of catch.

SCOOTERS

TYPE/CATEGORY: SCOOTER RACING

SETTING: CITY STREETS

REQUIREMENTS: HAMMER , NAILS, ONE SKATE, PIECE OF 2X4 , WOODEN MILK CRATE, NAILS

OBJECTIVE: CONSTRUCT AND RACE YOUR OWN SCOOTER

DESCRIPTION: There would come a time, during the warmer months of spring, summer or fall when the scooter building and racing season would appear. It was not a specific time of the calendar year but would probably be triggered by the appearance of the first scooter on the block. Building the scooters was as much fun as riding and racing them. They were very creative in design given that they were built of simple and readily available materials. The construction of the scooter was primarily a wooden milk crate nailed to a three foot piece of 2x4 with the halves of one skate at each end of the 2X4. Milk was delivered to the local grocery stores in wooden crates that measured about 12 inches wide by about 9 inches deep and about 18 inches long. The wooden crate was nailed to the 3 foot section of a 2x4 piece of wood such that the crate would form an "L" shape with the 2X4. To clarify, with the 2x4 placed flat on the ground, the builder would place the crate on its small side with the 18 inch length standing vertically and balanced on one end of the 2x4. The open end of the crate would face toward the other end of the 2x4 so that the first 9 inches of the 2x4 from one end was nailed to the bottom of the crate and centered with that bottom side of the crate. The nails were driven from the inside of the crate into the 2X4. The remaining 27 inches of the 2x4 served as the foot stand. At both ends of the 2x4, the half of a roller skate was also nailed. The common metal roller skate of the time was used. The individual skate was designed to fit over shoes with a clamp around the shoe toe and an ankle strap. Since they were also designed to fit all sizes of shoe, the skate was built with a front and back movable section. The sections could be moved apart to accommodate a larger shoe size and could be totally separated into two pieces, the front piece with the two front skate wheels and the back piece with the two rear wheels. These two pieces were then nailed to the 2x4. The front section of the skate was nailed to the front of the 2x4 and the rear section was nailed to the other end of the 2x4. By balancing the milk crate, and placing one foot on the 2x4 the scooter could be ridden. The other leg was used to propel the scooter and rider forward. Some kids would add special accessories such as two pieces of wood as handles that were nailed in an inverted "v" flat on the top of the crate to be used as hand grips, rather than leaning the hands on the side top edges of the crate. Some scooters were painted and decorated with colorful bottlecaps. Since the open end of the crate box was facing in toward the rider, a small panel of wood about half the size of the opening could be attached to enclose the lower half of the opening to form a small storage compartment. Scooters were raced on the city side streets with pride by their builders.

SCOOTERS

The wooden crate was nailed to the 3 foot section of a 2x4 piece of wood such that the crate would form an "L" shape with the 2X4. To clarify, with the 2x4 placed flat on the ground, the builder would place the crate on its small side with the 18 inch length standing vertically and balanced on one end of the 2x4.

SKATES

TYPE/CATEGORY: SKATING

SETTING: SCHOOL YARD ,PARK, SIDEWALK ,OR STREET

REQUIREMENTS: PAIR OF METAL ROLLER SKATES

OBJECTIVE: SKATING

DESCRIPTION: The roller skates of the time as described in the building of scooters, were made of metal and designed to fit over regular shoes. The individual skate was a one size fits all design that slide apart to accommodate larger or smaller shoe sizes as needed. The front movable section contained the two front wheels of the skate and the rear section of the skate contained the other two wheels. Once the correct size of the skate was found, a locking nut was tightened to keep the skate at that size. The front of the skate was held in place with toe clamps of which there were two designs. One type used smaller clamps that would grip the small edge of the shoes sole near the toe of the shoe. The more reliable toe clamps were larger and clamped around the entire toe of the shoe. The clamps were tightened with a skate key used to turn a threaded shaft that held the clamps tight against the shoe. At the back of the skate was a heel stop to which a mall leather ankle strap was attached. The skates were noisy and the wheels were made of metal also. Skating was smoother and more quiet on the asphalt side streets than on the concrete sidewalks. For a slight investment, the skate wheels could be replaced with "roller bearings" , i.e. a higher performance wheel. Roller skating was a very enjoyable pastime. Its not clear what marked the season for them, and it may have varied by neighborhood, but at certain times of the year, it was the current pastime for all the kids on the block. Many different activities were run on skates, such as tag, races, red light green light and even ring-a- leevio was a challenge on skates.

SKATES

For a slight investment, the skate wheels could be replaced with "roller bearings" , i.e. a higher performance wheel. Roller skating was a very enjoyable pastime. Its not clear what marked the season for them, and it may have varied by neighborhood, but at certain times of the year, it was the current pastime for all the kids on the block.

STICK BALL

TYPE/CATEGORY: BALL GAME

SETTING: SCHOOL YARD ,PARK, OR STREET

REQUIREMENTS: STICK, SPALDING BALL, BASEBALL GLOVES
WERE OPTIONAL

OBJECTIVE: SIMILAR TO BASEBALL

DESCRIPTION: A minimum of about three players per team was needed. Stick ball was probably one of the more popular block ball games. It was the inner city version of baseball adopted to the environment and was primarily played on the side streets between blocks. The side streets were more narrow and also experienced reduced automobile traffic. The two most important pieces of equipment were the stick ball bat and the rubber spaldeen ball. The bat was typically a wooden broom or mop handle of about 4 feet in length. It had no taper but wrapping the handle end of the stick with a fabric tape was a wise measure to ensure a better grip when swinging. This was doubly important for the players whose hair may have been slicked back with "Dixie Peach" as the stuff found its way into everything. The ball was called a spaldeen in generic terms, probably because of the predominant producer at the time. The spaldeen was a hollow rubber ball about the size and weight of a tennis ball but without the tennis ball felt covering. It was pink in color and though there were many imitations and all such were referred to as a spaldeen, the spaldeen made ball was superior in bounce and durability. A baseball glove could be either an asset or a liability depending on the condition. A new stiff glove was a disadvantage because the spaldeen was light and had a tendency to bounce out of the glove rather than bite into the glove as with the heavier more solid and hard baseball. An old soft glove was better for stick ball and with much of the pocket padding removed. The rules for stick ball would vary depending on the neighborhood and the field of play. When two teams from different neighborhoods played there was a need to reconcile these playing rules at the beginning to avoid disputes during the game. It was interesting to play and also watch different neighborhood teams at play. Their techniques and strategies varied. For example, because the spaldeen was a hollow and light ball, some batters would intentionally hit the ball very high into the air. The idea of this was that as the ball dropped it was more subject to wind shifting and catching a high fly ball was less predictable. Some batters hit the balls as low as possible. A low but hard hit spaldeen was also difficult to field and catch. The ball when hit hard would take on heavy spin and become egg shaped with a very unpredictable bounce on the asphalt pavement prior to an attempted catch. The bases and number of players also depended on the play field. A game with few players could be played with only two bases which were often two manhole covers. These were located in the center of the street at about 100 feet apart. There were various boundary markers such as light posts, cars, fire escapes, fire hydrants, etc. With more players per team additional bases were drawn with chalk on the street. There was rarely a pitcher used in the game of stick ball. Instead the batter (if right handed) holding the bat in his right hand and the spaldeen in his left hand would through the ball in front of the bat at about his height and then swing at the ball either before it hit the ground or on the first bounce of the ball when it reached about waist height. The rules where broadly consistent with baseball, i.e. 3 strikes per out, three outs per inning, and nine innings. Depending on the playing field width, number and proximity of cars, posts, buildings, fire escapes etc., the rules for a fair ball needed to be set early in the game. Since the side streets were narrow compared to a regular baseball field hitting the ball into fire escapes or sides of buildings was easy, and the rules would need to be clarified when such were either fouls, automatic doubles or otherwise. It was an enjoyable spectator sport.

STICK BALL

A baseball glove could be either an asset or a liability depending on the condition. A new stiff glove was a disadvantage because the spaldeen was light and had a tendency to bounce out of the glove rather than bite into the glove as with the heavier more solid and hard baseball. An old soft glove was better for stick ball and with much of the pocket padding removed.

STOOP BALL

TYPE/CATEGORY: BALL GAME

SETTING: STOOP IN FRONT OF AN APARTMENT BUILDING

REQUIREMENTS: AT LEAST THREE PLAYERS, AND A SPALDEEN
BALL

OBJECTIVE: TO REMAIN AT STOOP BATTING AS LONG AS
POSSIBLE

DESCRIPTION: One version of the game was similar to the "flies are up"
game previously described in that the field player to catch three fly balls would
win his turn at the stoop. Stoops were concrete and/or brick steps that extended
from the buildings front entrance down to the street level. The number of stoop
steps depended on how high from the street level the entrance was. Stoops
ranged from about two steps to about ten steps. In the city of Philadelphia it is
said that in the early colonial days, the number of stoop steps corresponded to
the level of financial status of the residents. After choosing, one player would
win the stoop batting position and the other players would play the field. The
stoop batter would face the stoop and the ball was hit down against the concrete
steps. On the rebound the ball would fly into the street in front of the building
where the field players positioned themselves. The ball typically hit the stoop

between the vertical and horizontal faces of the first and second steps. Catching the outer corner edge of a step would result in the hardest and highest rebound. The game could be played with variation, including the running of bases if teams were set up. The three most common versions were 1. "flies are up" stoop ball. In this game after catching three fly balls, the field player won his turn at the stoop. 2. Running bases, where teams were established and bases were drawn on the ground with chalk. In this game the rules were otherwise similar to stick ball. 3. Baseball bounce rules were used in this third version as in the boxball baseball game described previously. For this game the ball would need to pass a certain point on a fly and then for each bounce before being caught or fielded, a base was scored. For example if the ball bounced twice before being stopped or caught by a field player, the stoop batter had scored a double. If the ball was dropped by a fielder, the number of bounces also counted as a corresponding number of bases scored. The scoring was a bit complex and required keeping track of the number of "men on base" from the prior turn.

<u>STOOP BALL</u>

The three most common versions were 1. "flies are up" stoop ball. In this game after catching three fly balls, the field player won his turn at the stoop. 2. Running bases, where teams were established and bases were drawn on the ground with chalk. In this game the rules were otherwise similar to stick ball. 3. Baseball bounce rules were used in this third version as in the box ball baseball game described previously

TAG

TYPE/CATEGORY: RUNNING TAG

SETTING: SIDEWALK, **PLAYGROUND**

REQUIREMENTS: NO SPECIAL EQUIPMENT

OBJECTIVE: TO TAG OTHER PLAYERS IN CHASE.

DESCRIPTION: The game was a simple pastime. A group of kids would choose and the losing player became the tagger and all other the "taggees". The tagger would chase the other players. Boundaries could be set if desired, within which all players had to confine themselves. Once tagged players would join in the chase to tag the remaining players. The last player to remain untagged was the winner. An alternative version was to pass the tagging responsibility with the tag. In other words, once tagged the player became the tagger until he tagged another player. In confined boundaries, speed, agility and the ability to dodge and fast zig zag running were survival.

TAG
Once tagged players would join in the chase to tag the remaining players. The last player to remain untagged was the winner.

TOPS

TYPE/CATEGORY: TOP SPINNING

SETTING: SCHOOL YARD ,PARK, OR STREET

REQUIREMENTS: AT LEAST TWO PLAYERS ,CHALK, TOPS AND CHORD.

OBJECTIVE: TO OUT SPIN THE OTHER PLAYERS TOPS

DESCRIPTION: The game required a certain amount of skill in winding, releasing and handling the spinning tops of the time. Though it was seasonal, top season appeared at different times of the year, either when a few of the neighborhood kids brought out their prior year's tops or when the local candy store got in a new supply of shiny new tops. The tops were made of wood with a metal tip imbedded at the narrow end to the tapered top. The wide end of the top was about 1 1/2 inches in diameter and the top was about two inches in height. It was tapered down to a narrow end just a bit wider than the inserted metal tip or spike. The metal tip was about the thickness of a penny nail and extended beyond the top about 1/4 of an inch and had a small metal ridge where it joined the wooden top. This acted as a stop to keep the starting windings of the cord in position. Winding the top tightly and neatly was tricky and required skill. Skill was required in winding, holding the top for release, arm and wrist action on the release, and picking up the top while still spinning. The cord was about the thickness of a single speaker or common bell wire. The top was thrown into a spin on the ground in front and a few feet away from the player. It could be thrown or released either over hand or under hand. In either case, had to be thrown with specific arm and wrist action as when pitching a baseball with side spin. Spin was put on the release and the cord would be retracted with a jerking motion to ensure that it was clear of the top before the top hit the ground. The effective combination of all these things increased the spinning time or duration which was an objective for some versions of the game. For example one version of the game required all the players to spin their tops at the same time. The first top to stop spinning unfortunately became a target top. It would be placed in the center of a chalk drawn circle of about a foot in diameter. The other players would then take turns and aim their tops at the target top. Which would stay a target until it was hit out of the circle. Once out of the circle, the players would again spin simultaneously their tops to determine the next top to go into the target circle. Other targets such as coins or bottle caps were also used in play. Another skill used in play was picking up a spinning top either by hand or with the string. The open hand was used to scoop up the spinning top and the top could continue spinning in the player's open palm to be dropped down against the target top. Rarely was a top split and though it could happen more frequently the tops were worse for the wear full of notches and gauges. If rules allowed, the losing player was permitted to substitute an old beat up top into the target circle if his spinning top was new.

<u>TOPS</u>

Winding the top tightly and neatly was tricky and required skill. Skill was required in winding, holding the top for release, arm and wrist action on the release, and picking up the top while still spinning.

WATER BALLOONS

TYPE/CATEGORY: PASTIME

SETTING: ANY WHERE ON THE BLOCK

REQUIREMENTS: A SUPPLY OF BALLOONS AND ACCESS TO A WATER FAUCET.

OBJECTIVE: TO THROW BALLOONS FILLED WITH WATER.

DESCRIPTION: This pastime was played during the warmer months of the year. Balloons were purchased in the local candy store and filled with water. They could then be used in playing "hot potato" were the water filled balloon was tossed among the kids. The idea was to avoid dropping the balloon or breaking it. The best size for tossing was about the diameter of a softball. Water balloons were also used in water balloon fights. They were thrown by kids at each other. Unsuspecting kids were chased and at times a water balloon would be thrown from a roof or apartment window and land on an unsuspecting passer by.

WATER BALLOONS
They could then be used in playing "hot potato" were the water filled balloon was tossed among the kids. The idea was to avoid dropping the balloon or breaking it. The best size for tossing was about the diameter of a softball.

WATERPUMP (JOHNNY PUMP)

TYPE/CATEGORY: PASTIME

SETTING: STREET NEAR A FIRE HYDRANT

REQUIREMENTS: WRENCH, TIN CAN

OBJECTIVE: SPRAYING WATER.

DESCRIPTION: This was an occasional summer pastime though not totally within ordinance. On very hot summer days, someone would remove the cap to one of the two outlets of the fire hydrant. A wrench was needed to turn the water on top of the pump. Kids would jump and frolic on the street within the spray of the water. A tin can about the size of a coffee can with both lids removed could be used as a deflecting device to raise the spray of the water. Because of its pressure the pump's spray was extensive and powerful and could easily reach 50 to 100 feet. This posed a real threat to the unsuspecting motorist with an open window or convertible. The opening of a water pump would typically last for about an hour or so until the local police patrol or fire department showed up to shut off the water. In later years special perforated caps were installed on the pumps. This controlled the drop in water pressure and served as a water sprinkler during hot summer days for the neighborhood kids.

WATERPUMP (JOHNNY PUMP)

This posed a real threat to the unsuspecting motorist with an open window or convertible. The opening of a water pump would typically last for about an hour or so until the local police patrol of fire department showed up to shut off the water

PAPER AIRPLANES

TYPE/CATEGORY: PASTIME

SETTING: ANYWHERE

REQUIREMENTS: PIECE OF PAPER STANDARD 8 ½ X 11 ½

OBJECTIVE: DESIGN A FLIGHT EFFICIENT PAPER AIRPLANE

DESCRIPTION: Designing and flying paper airplanes was another fun pastime. It was particularly engaging because the architect/designer had the ability to experiment with various configurations and shapes and test the airborne efficiency and performance of these different designs. The fact that the plane was constructed by merely folding a piece of paper made construction and experimentation fairly simple. Performance was measured primarily in terms of distance, speed, and flight duration. The paper airplanes were thrown by hand either from an elevated position such as a balcony, or were thrown either up into the air or at about shoulder level (as in a room or hall where there may not have been high ceiling clearance). When more than one player was involved, the planes were flown to see which would either fly the farthest or to see which would glide the longest. Design was dependent on the objective i.e. for distance a longer and narrower construction was typical, while wider wing span was needed for extended gliding. The optimal design would accomplish both distance and duration. The rules of competition would vary and at times duration would be accomplished by throwing the plane from the ground up vertically into the air. By making slight adjustments to the airfoils the plane could be made to glide in a circular pattern a number of times before landing. The following is a typical design that accomplished both distance and duration.

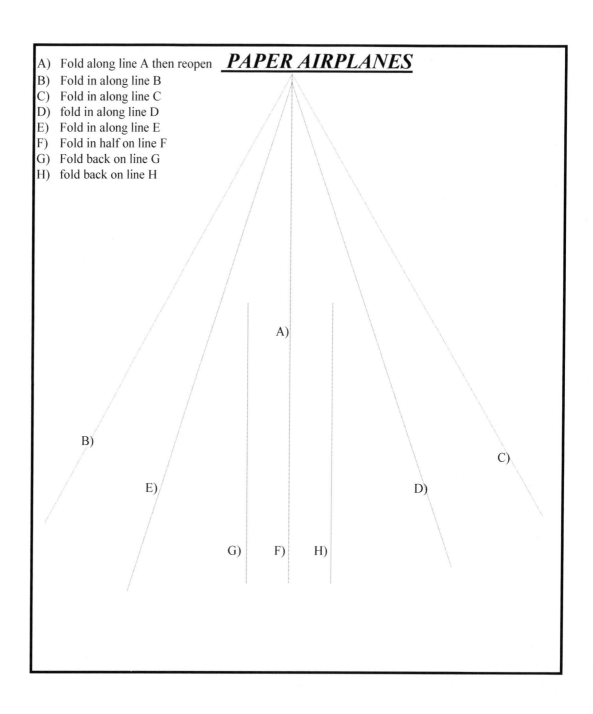

A) Fold along line A then reopen
B) Fold in along line B
C) Fold in along line C
D) fold in along line D
E) Fold in along line E
F) Fold in half on line F
G) Fold back on line G
H) fold back on line H

PAPER AIRPLANES

The Brylcreem Strikeout

*Unfortunately, a "little dab" didn't do
this stickball player much good at all
on this day in 1960.*

*(THE ILLUSTRATION BY CLIFF WIRTH OF THE CHICAGO SUN TIMES AS WELL AS THE
FOLLOWING ARTICLE BY THE AUTHOR WERE FEATURED IN **REMINISCE MAGAZINE**
DESCRIBING ONE OF THE MANY STREET GAME ADVENTURES RECALLED
BY THE AUTHOR DURING THE 1960'S)*

THE BRYLCREEM STRIKEOUT

As I recall it, my "Brylcreem strikeout" happened in the summer of 1960.

Our stickball games on Cauldwell Avenue in the Bronx usually began in the afternoons. Summer mornings were for sleeping late, or for pitching pennies or trading comic books and baseball cards.

Cauldwell Avenue was a narrow one-way street with cars parked on both sides, and many of the neighborhood buildings had shops on the first floor.

There was Pepe's Candy Store (where you could get "egg creams" and other delights), a dry cleaner and Pablo's Grocery Store (Pablo was my dad).

PLAYING FIELD WAS TIGHT

The narrow street made for some unusual rules of play. Because the field was so elongated, we'd use two bases. One manhole cover was "home", and the other base another manhole cover 200 feet farther down the street.

Because of the number and proximity of cars, posts, buildings, fire escapes, etc., the rules for a fair ball needed to be set early in the game. The two pieces of equipment used were the rubber "spaldeen" ball and a stickball bat. The spaldeen was hollow and about the size of a tennis ball, but without the fuzz covering.

Since the ball was so light, some batters (like my friend, Thomas) tried to hit it higher than the rooftops. That way the wind would catch the light ball and make it harder to catch. Thomas was so fast that by the time the fielders got control of the ball, he was already back home.

Other batters hit the ball as low as possible. A hard-hit low ball was tough to field because it would take on a heavy spin and become egg-shaped, causing unpredictable bounces on the asphalt.

The stickball bat was typically a wooden broom or mop handle about 4 feet long with the handle often wrapped with some sort of fabric tape. Unfortunately, that was not the case on this day.

I should now mention the Brylcreem was undoubtedly "cool" for us 16-year olds back then. The pompadour was the hair-style of the day—although crew cuts were popular, too.

Either way, you used Brylcreem. You couldn't get your pompadour to stay without it, and for some reason, you also needed to slick it over your crew cut.

On that particular day, we weren't using a pitcher. The batter threw the ball up into the air with his left hand (if right handed) and either hit the ball when it was in the air or on the first bounce.

Smooth Move!

When I threw the ball up and swung the bat, I must have just combed my hair or run my hand over it to slick it back, because of my first swing, the *bat* (instead of the ball) took flight!

It flew over a parked car and directly into the glass entrance door of an apartment building, hitting head on and shattering it!

Within seconds, all the other guys scrammed. Meanwhile, I just stood there. People up and down the block always watched those games, and since everybody in the neighborhood knew me, it didn't make much sense to run.

I can't recall now whether the building super came down or not, but what probably happened was that someone ran into the grocery store and said, "Hey, Pablo, your son just busted the window down at 816!"

You can bet I delivered a lot of groceries that summer to pay for that smashed glass!

*Two past Urbanites who reminisce about their youth in the city of
these games provide their commentary below:*

Interview with Mr. Garrett J. Cronin

*(At the time of the first version of this compendium, the following interview was conducted. The
dates and corresponding references, which may not be current with the date of the book's current
edition, have been kept as originally recorded)*

When PAR Enterprises and its associates sought to develop an appropriate
testimonial to the Official Compendium Of Inner City Street Games, some of
our collaborators suggested interviewing a community leader that both played
these games as a youngster and became involved heavily with the youth of our
inner cities. Those who know Mr. Garrett J. Cronin would agree that he is the
ideal candidate to speak on this subject as is evident from his background, his
endeavors and the enthusiasm for these games that he conveys in the following
interview conducted by John F. Recchia of PAR Enterprises, Inc..

Background: Mr. Garrett ("GARY") J. Cronin was born and raised in New
York City and as a child and teenager was a very active participant and skillful
athlete of the inner city street games. Mr. Cronin is the founder of Cronin
Enterprises, Inc. and Vice President of International Business Development
Fleming Packaging Corporation. He attended Holy Trinity grammar school, Rice
High School in Manhattan and Iona college and is a graduate of New York
University's graphic arts/design program. Mr. Cronin married for 36 + years,
with 6 children and 6 grandchildren. His community activities include being a

member of the Knights of Columbus, Knights of Malta, and Knights of St. Patrick. Mr. Cronin also served as Vice President of the Board of Directors for the CYO - Archdiocese of NY (and has been a board member for over 30 years). He is also President of EDUCAGE, a not for profit special education youth program in White Plains, New York and has served as past director of Little League Baseball and a chairman for the Cardinal's Appeal - Archdiocese of New York for Our Lady Of Mt. Carmel in Elmsford, New York. PAR Enterprises is fortunate to have the opportunity to capture many of Mr. "Gary" Cronin's thoughts and knowledge of the wonderful legacy of the inner city street games in the following interview.

John: Gary, as many others have, you also responded very favorably to the **Official Compendium Inner City Street Games**. We felt that your interview would be of value as testimonial to the book because of your long standing support and involvement with the youth of the inner city and also because you were very active in these games as a youngster. What neighborhood was the backdrop for these games when you were a youngster.

Gary: As a young teenager during the post war 1950's I lived in New York City on the west side of Manhattan on 83st and Columbus Avenue. It was an exciting time and the neighborhood had a rich diversity of ethnic backgrounds. The games became one of the ways of developing camaraderie and affiliation among the different groups.

John: Your continued involvement and leadership in youth organizations over the years reflects your belief in the value of the camaraderie that sports and inner city street games develops among the young. Please describe some of your activities with these organizations.

Gary: Well I've been involved as a director and Vice President of the CYO which operates in ten counties throughout the archdiocese of New York and I obviously believe strongly in what an organization like the CYO represents. My activities included directing fund raising programs and recognition programs such as the annual Club Of Champions Dinner. The John V. Mara Sports Award has been presented at these dinners to many famous sports figures such as Lou Holtz, Yogi Berra, Tommy Lasorta, "Dr. J." Julius Irving, Phil Simms, George Martin and Casey Stengel. I think that one of the best ways of describing my interests with the young and sports is the fact that over the years there probably isn't one gymnasium of the CYO parish schools in the Bronx or Manhattan, that I have not visited either as a coach or a player. I think that including Westchester County, I may have visited approximately 250 gymnasiums either as a participant or coach.

John: What was it about the Compendium that first caught your attention?

Gary: What really caught my attention is that the book captures a legacy of wonderful, fun filled activities, and, as mentioned in the book, these are activities which were **<u>real, three dimensional</u>** and challenging as opposed to today's virtual reality pastimes. It was a nostalgic "pick me up" . I've been excited about the book since I first saw it in draft form and I think this would be a wonderful item to be included in various programs, like fund raisers among other organizations such as PAL, PSAL, high schools, grammar schools, etc. I have talked in general with people from Baltimore, Philadelphia, Chicago, Los Angeles, Detroit, Boston, and the reaction has been great. The games were quickly identified by those I spoke to and it brought back memories to them of great times in the past. Even today some of the games are still played throughout the various cities in the US. The games are timeless. They are excellent physical activities requiring ingenuity, creativity, agility, and team work. These games train the mind to understand the physical world unlike today's hi-tech virtual reality games that lack the reality of physics and "gravity".

John: The array and complement of inner city games was extensive, and though the rules, and sometimes names, of the games varied among cities and even neighborhoods, the games remained broadly consistent. What were some of your favorite games and in what neighborhoods were they played?

Gary: Well most of the games like stickball were played in all the neighborhoods and in all the other cities. I enjoyed so many games that it would be difficult to say which was my favorite. Each game had its own appeal and type of excitement and challenge whether it was Street Hockey, Pitching Pennies, Box Baseball, Three Man Basketball, One On One, Johnny On The

Pony, Tops, Water Balloons, Tops, or even Potsy. Even Potsy was a challenge for us "jocks" because it required good balance, and eye-hand coordination. Another of my more favorites was stoop ball which had various versions. Stoop ball was so typical of the inner city because "stoops" themselves were virtually non-existent outside of the cities. This was a game that evolved out of a natural inner city "prop" and to get different trajectories with the ball, one had to strike the stoop step at different points. Another game that I enjoyed was box baseball which was played again with the rubber spaldeen ball or "pinky" as we called it. In box baseball, as described in the book, the square outlines on the concrete sidewalks were used as the playing field. Success in box baseball depended on the different spins that could be put on the ball by the pitcher. This game was great fun and also one of my favorites.

John: You also recall the major stick ball tournaments that were held when one neighborhood challenged another,…can you tell us a bit about these 'Major" stick ball games.?

Gary: We always felt that we were the best in the world, and our world in those days was inscribed by about ten square blocks. On occasion there was the opportunity to play someone beyond our ten square block world. Such games were a major event. They would be held either on a Saturday or Sunday afternoon and the neighborhoods would prepare for these big games. And it was stiff competition because it was typically the more senior or seasoned and "older" (late teens or early 20's") players that played in these inter-neighborhood tournaments. We would travel as much as a mile or two to these big events. I remember going to the west 96 Street and east 96 Street neighborhoods for these games or to east Harlem on 116 Street. These games were such a neighborhood "happening" and there was always a big build up to these games that at times there would be neighborhood wagers on the outcome.

John: Some of the terms that you recall as being typical to these games are "DO OVER", "NEW BATTING ORDER" , " THE BIG GUY", etc. ….Can you elaborate on these and other terms that you recall were standard jargon with special meanings?

Gary: Certainly some of these terms were specific to a neighborhood or type of play while other terms had general application. For example, the "Big Guy" in our terms referred to the most influential player on our "Block", which many times was literally a big guy. The "Big Guy" controlled the games in many different ways. If he didn't like the way the game was going he would call an "NBO" or New Batting Order. The big guy could change the rules or call for a "Do Over" which required a replay for some unknown or obscure technicality. "Fins" was a term used for declaring a time out. Another curious term was "Chicky" . This was the term that a was used by a posted "look out" to alert everyone that a policeman was coming. It wasn't that the games were life threatening, but some of the activities like throwing water balloons from a roof top or opening up the Johnny Pump on a hot summer afternoon could get a kid in trouble or at least a warning from the cops.

John: There were also more formally, organized games, such as the 3 Man Basketball Championships…How were these games played and what are some of your favorite stories about them?

Gary: In 1954 and 1955, a three-man basketball championship was organized to raise funds to help St. Elizabeth's due to a fire that had burnt down the school. During that tournament, myself, Charles Kavanagh (now Monsignor Kavanagh, Director of Development for the Archdiocese of New York) and Tony Estella entered the tournament and we took on the "world" . We won nine straight games. Which were very exciting twenty single point games , i.e. the first team to make 20 goals won the game. In all nine games I didn't score one basket, as I focused on assist playing, but our opposing teams also didn't score but one basket. Monsignor Kavanagh was just "on fire" in those games. I have fond memories of those games and in particular of Tony Estella , a Philippine American, from the west side who subsequently gave up his life in the military during the Viet Nam War. The annual foul line shooting contest was another memorable event. This event was held on George Washington's Birthday at St. Ann's Gymnasium on Lexington Avenue in the vicinity of 76th and 77th Streets in Manhattan. The best foul shooters from each of the parishes would compete. One needed 6 out of ten goals to qualify. In this one particular year, Monsignor Kavanagh qualified with 10 out of 10 and I fed him on the line. What was unique about that competition is that Monsignor Kavanagh had to go through an elimination process of four rounds of "Shoot Outs" of 25 tries each with another player. At the end of the fourth round, Monsignor Kavanagh, won the contest by one goal with 96 out of 100 successful goals. In my mind that will always be one "for the books".

John: What were some of the various props and playing equipment that you recall and how were they used ?

Gary: Well the stick ball bat was your mother's "old" wooden broom handle with the broom sheared off at the end (we'd use the sewer openings to snap off the broom heads). The spaldeen as described in the book or the "pinky" as it was also referred to, was standard equipment for many of the games which were played by both genders. We'd spend hours playing a wide variety of games with a spaldeen. In "field hockey" the "puck" was fashioned and rolled from wire. Heavy shoes were a must, as protection and the game was played on the street with man-hole covers about 100 feet apart being the goals. Even the small wooden "popsicle" stick that supported the ice cream bars was a great prop. It was used in the ball bounce-popsicle stick game described in the book.

John: One last question, Gary,…who would you recommend this book to and do you think its only pleasing nostalgic reminiscing for boomers or all ages?

Gary: I would recommend this book not only to those who want to remember the past but to parents and grand parents who would like to pass on this fun - filled legacy to their children and grandchildren. I believe the book has excellent appeal with boomers, many of which have moved into the suburban surrounding areas of the inner city. Today's youth could benefit from learning and playing these games. The book could be a great reference for schools, youth organizations, etc. and the games are a great way to get youngsters out to experience reality, gravity, energy and the camaraderie of these very creative sporting activities,…it would give them a **break from their "virtual reality" hi tech environment.** The book can be a valuable tool in youth ministry in helping young people learn the value of team work, camaraderie, and problem solving through games and sports in the real world. I think that preserving these games is very important, and I salute PAR Enterprises, and its associates for taking the initiative and recording these games in an official compendium and I look forward to volume two of the Compendium

Bill Wagner , retired Senior Vice President - Grubb & Ellis C0. And "Bronxite" reminisces about the games and living in the Bronx, New York as a youth……..STROLLING THROUGH THE MIND OF A BRONXITE. I'll just mention much that made growing up in The Bronx a joy. These include stickball, stoopball, Johnny on a pony, marble gambling, snow forts, pickup basketball, football and baseball, the May 1st Maypole at P.S. 70,bicycling throughout the Borough without fear at ten years of age. And one mustn't forget "spin the bottle".

…And so much more. Most of the best high schools in New York - Cardinal Hayes, Taft, Science, Roosevelt, DeWitt Clinton and others.

Note that having once been a Bronxite, regardless of the years removed ,one is always a Bronxite.

We must acknowledge the extreme significance of The Bronx in that it is the only geographic identity, except for The United States, which identity importantly preceded by "The".

Having dispensed with the heralded recognition, permit me to stroll through this wonderfully geographic entity. Strolling in The Bronx commences with the grandest boulevard in New York City and, perhaps, the entire country. Where else can one, shortly after beginning their stroll, turn their head to the left and see the Great Yankee Stadium, home of "The Champs". Strolling the Concourse from beginning to end offers a mix of parks and gardens, magnificent apartment houses of all historic styles beautifully executed, public buildings, perhaps the best shopping district outside of Manhattan, the home of Edgar Allen Poe, more wonderfully executed architecture and ending at another at another grand boulevard, Moshulu Parkway and the beginning of the spectacular VanCortlandt park.

The Bronx could be named the borough of parks. Commencing with the grandest of all - Bronx Botanical Gardens, with the adjoining Bronx Zoo, stands out as worldwide institutions. Adding numerous parks such as Van Cortlandt, Claremont, Crotona and others with their pools, stone outcroppings for climbing, bountifully equipped playgrounds (thanks to litigation fears largely removed) , makes The Bronx a most playful paradise.

Incidentally, The Paradise was the magnificent Loew's movie theatre, grandly bedecked with a ceiling resembling a starlight sky. It also housed the "largest necking venue" in the city. And across the Grand Concourse was the venerable Krum's ice cream parlor. Yeah we know Queens had Jahn's, which later opened a Bronx outpost, bur nothing was better than sitting at the Krum's counter watching your "soda jerk" peers whip up the ice cream concoctions. I say peers because many Bronx youths had their first job experience scooping Krum's ice creams.

...... Yes - Growing up in The Bronx was a place never duplicated and, unfortunately, not likely to be repeated. I am blessed having had the opportunity to enjoy the city and neighborhood games at the time of my formative years.

==

PAR ENTERPRISES, INC. AND ITS ASSOCIATES TRUST THAT YOU HAVE ENJOYED READING AND REMINISCING ABOUT INNER-CITY FUN AND GAMES.

BECAUSE OF THE VARIABILITY OF NAMES AND RULES WHICH AT TIMES DIFFERED EVEN FROM NEIGHBORHOOD TO NEIGHBORHOOD , VOLUME ONE OF THE OFFICIAL GUIDE TO INNER-CITY STREET GAMES HAS PRESENTED SOME VERSIONS OF THE GAMES WITH NAMES IN SOME CASES SPELLED PHONETICALLY IN THE ABSENCE OF STANDARDIZED SPELLING.